Constructive Abandonment
by Michael Dumontier and Neil Farber

Drawn & Quarterly, Montréal

Entire contents © copyright 2011 by Michael Dumontier and Neil Farber. All rights reserved. No part of this book (except small portions for review purposes) may be reproduced in any form without written permission from Michael Dumontier, Neil Farber or Drawn & Quarterly. Drawn & Quarterly Post Office Box 48056 Montreal, Quebec Canada H2V 4S8. www.drawnandquarterly.com First Hardcover edition: May 2011. 10 9 8 7 6 5 4 3 2 1; Printed in Singapore. Library and Archives Canada Cataloguing in Publication Dumontier, Michael, 1974; -Constructive Abandonment / Michael Dumontier and Neil Farber. ISBN 978-1-77046-045-4; I. Farber, Neil, 1975- II. Title. PN6733.D84C65 2011 741.5'971   C2010-907564-1; Distributed in the United States by: Farrar, Straus & Giroux 18 West 18th Street New York, NY 10001, Call Toll-free: 888.330.8477 ext. 6540, www.fsgbooks.com; Distributed in Canada by: Raincoast Books 2440 Viking Way Richmond, BC V6V 1N2 Orders: 1-800-663-5714, www.raincoast.com customerservice@raincoast.com; Distributed in the UK by: Publishers Group UK 8 The Arena, Mollison Avenue, Enfield EN3 7NL Tel: 020 8804 0400, www.pguk.co.uk; Drawn & Quarterly acknowledges the financial support of the Government of Canada through the Canada Book Fund and the Canada Council for the Arts for our publishing activities and for support of this edition.

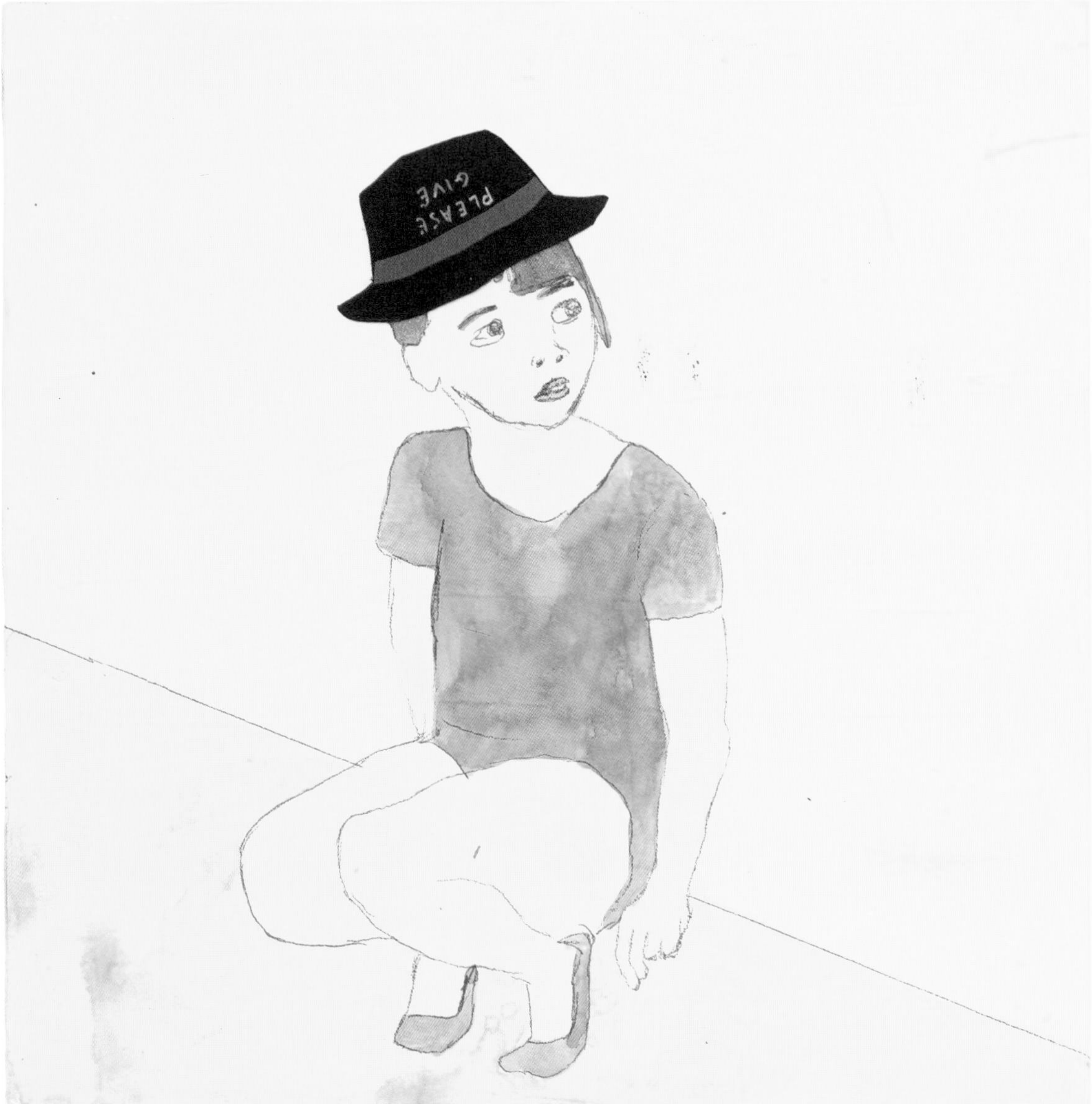
PLEASE
GIVE

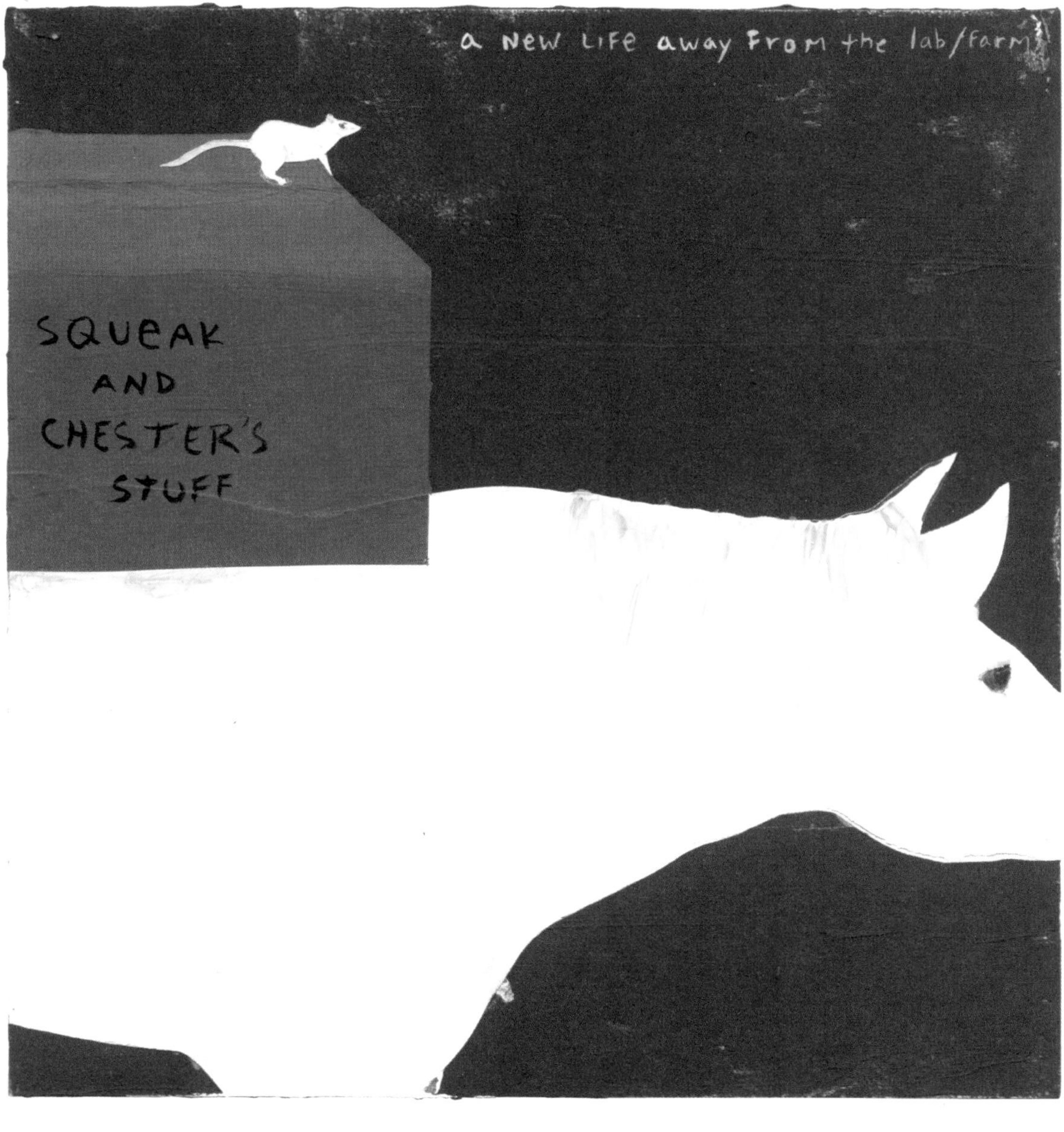
a new life away from the lab/farm
SQUEAK
AND
CHESTER'S
STUFF

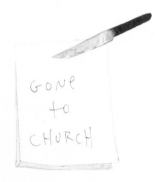

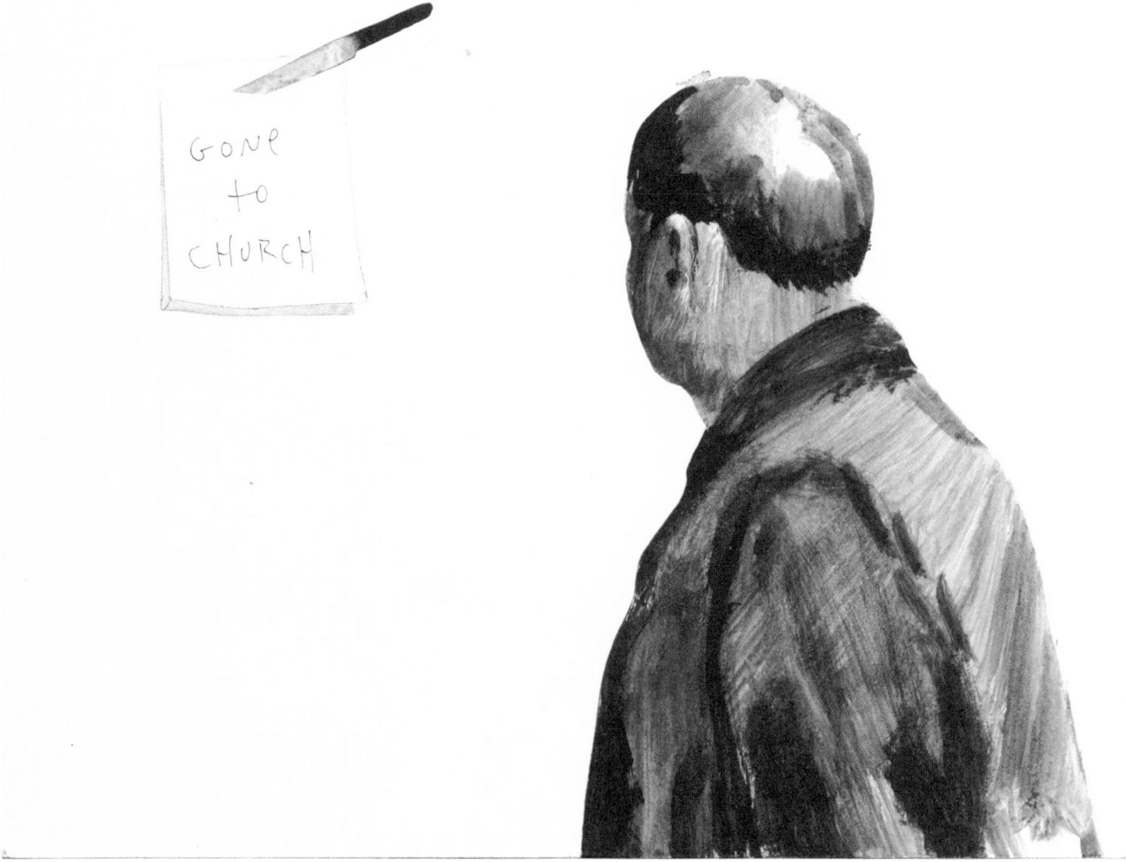
GONE
to
CHURCH

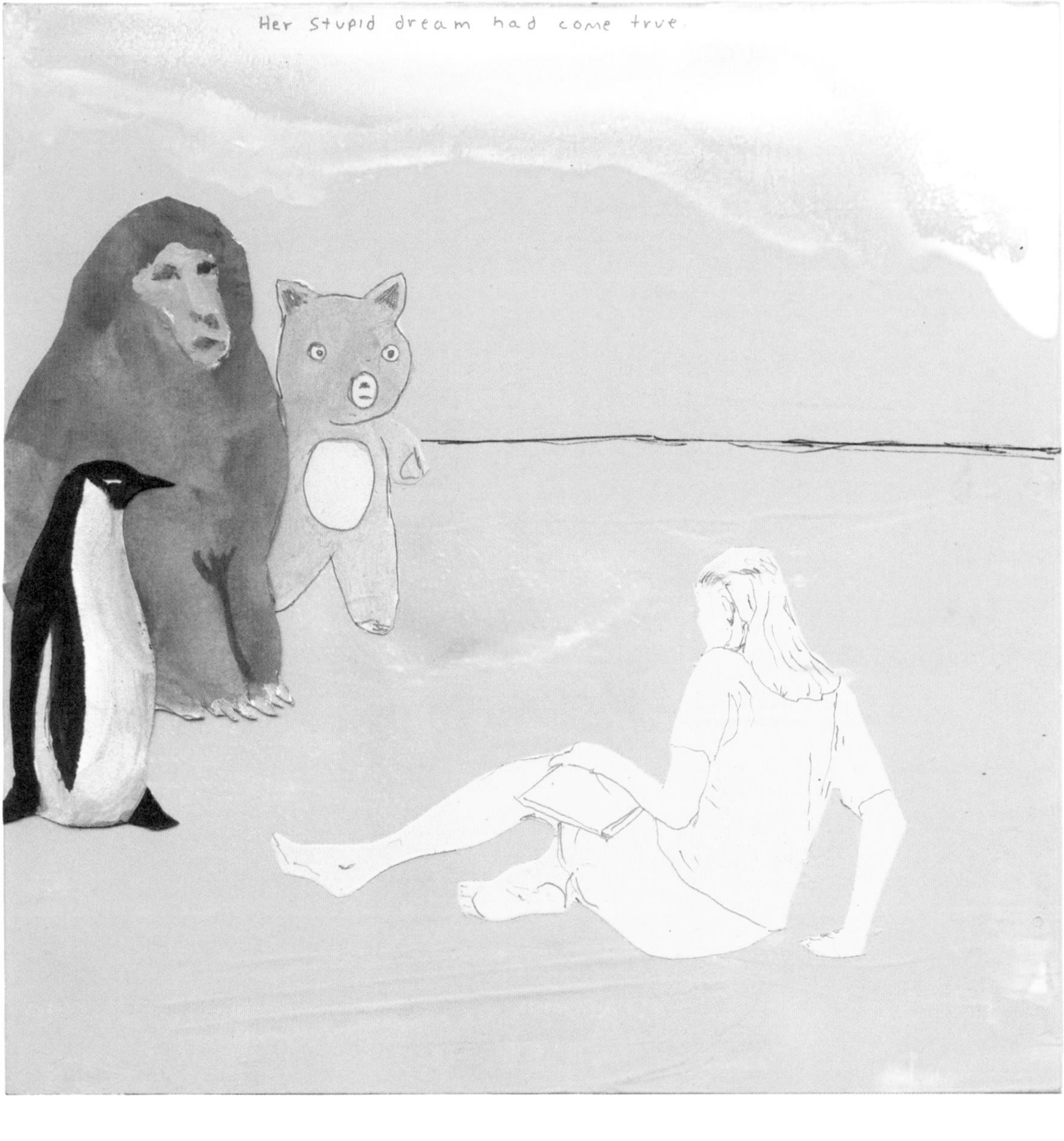
Her stupid dream had come true.

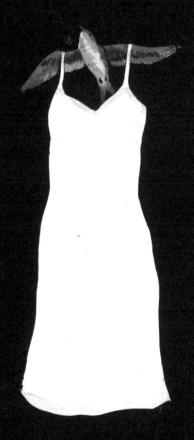

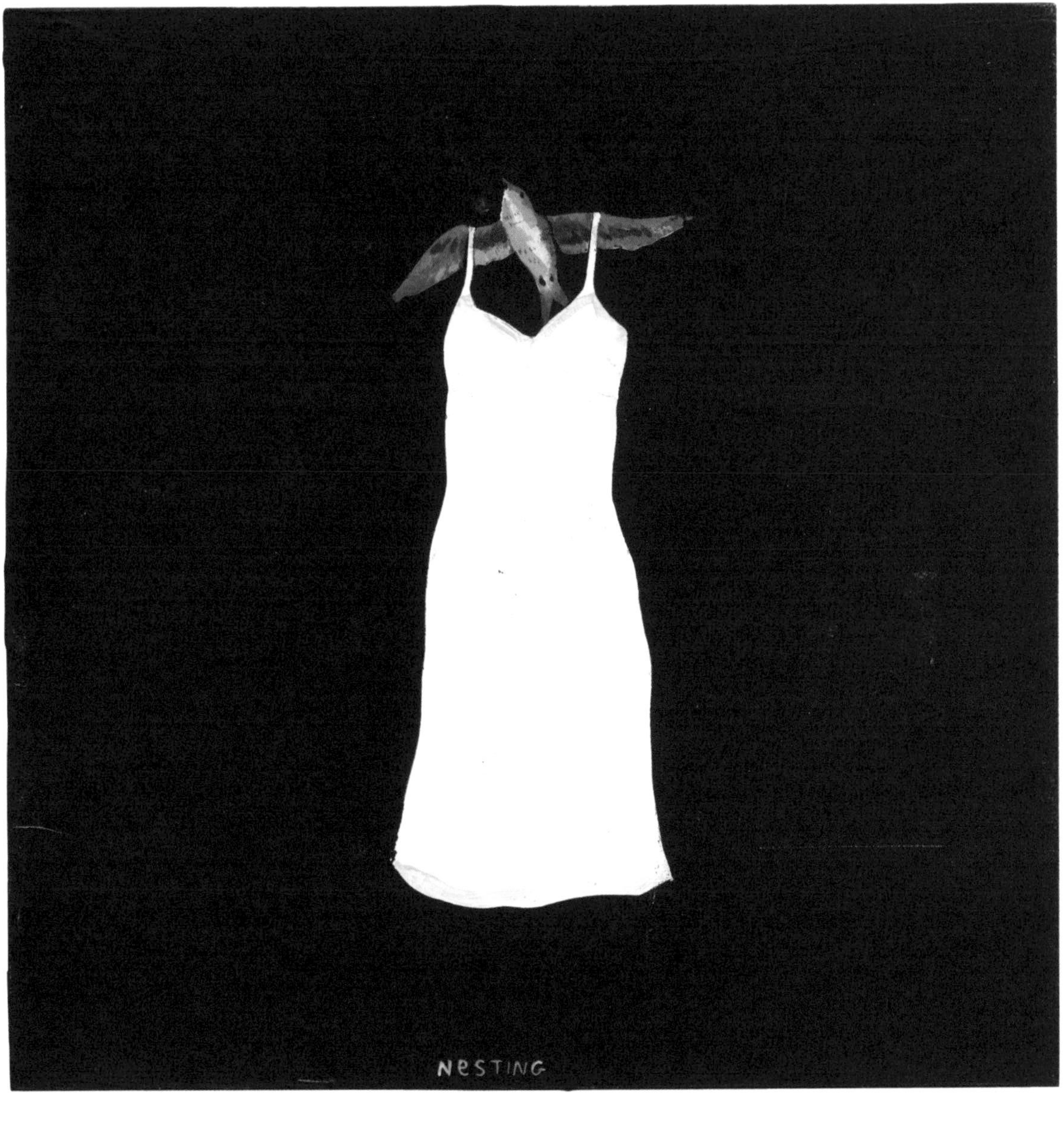

NESTING

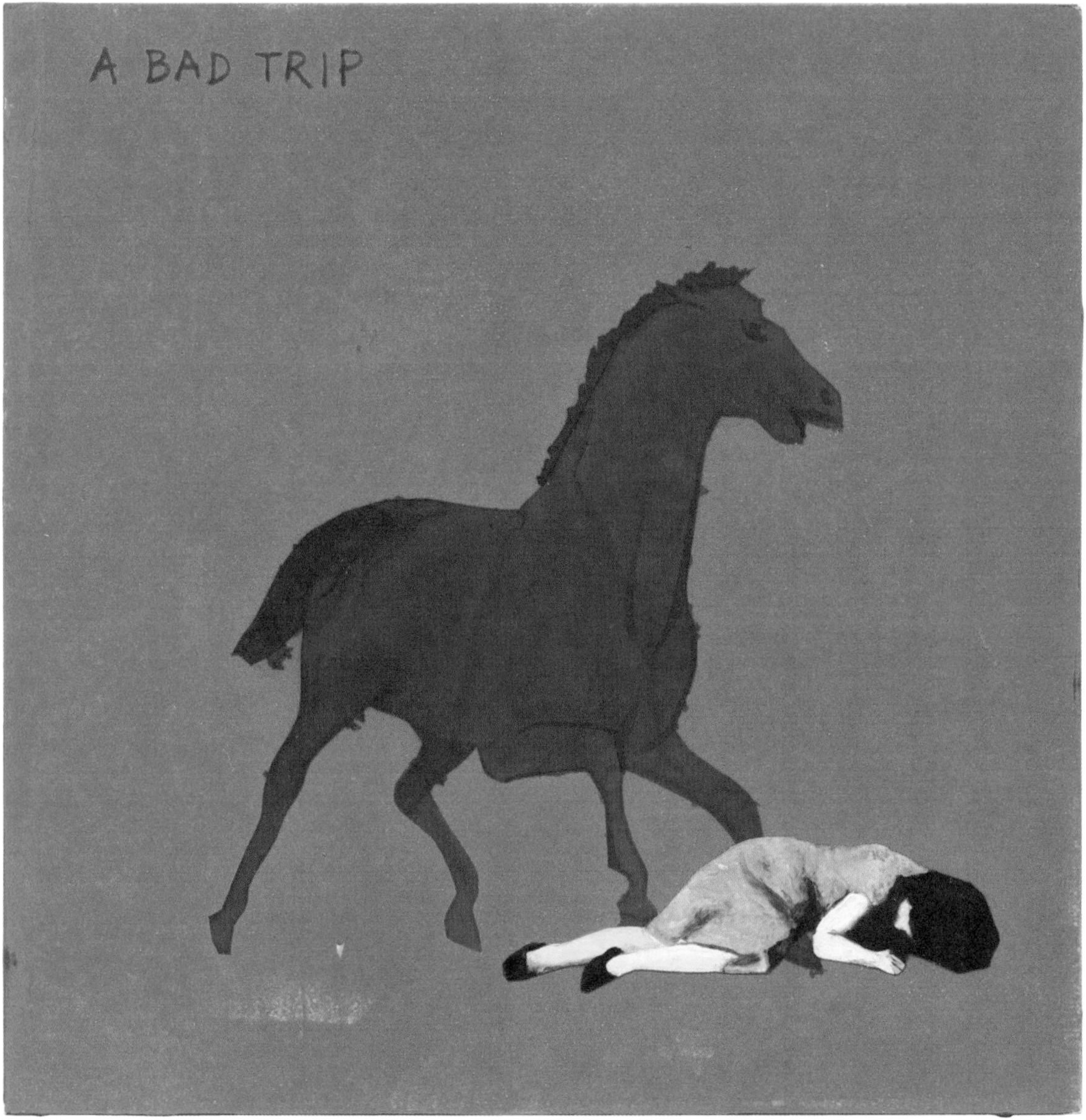
A BAD TRIP

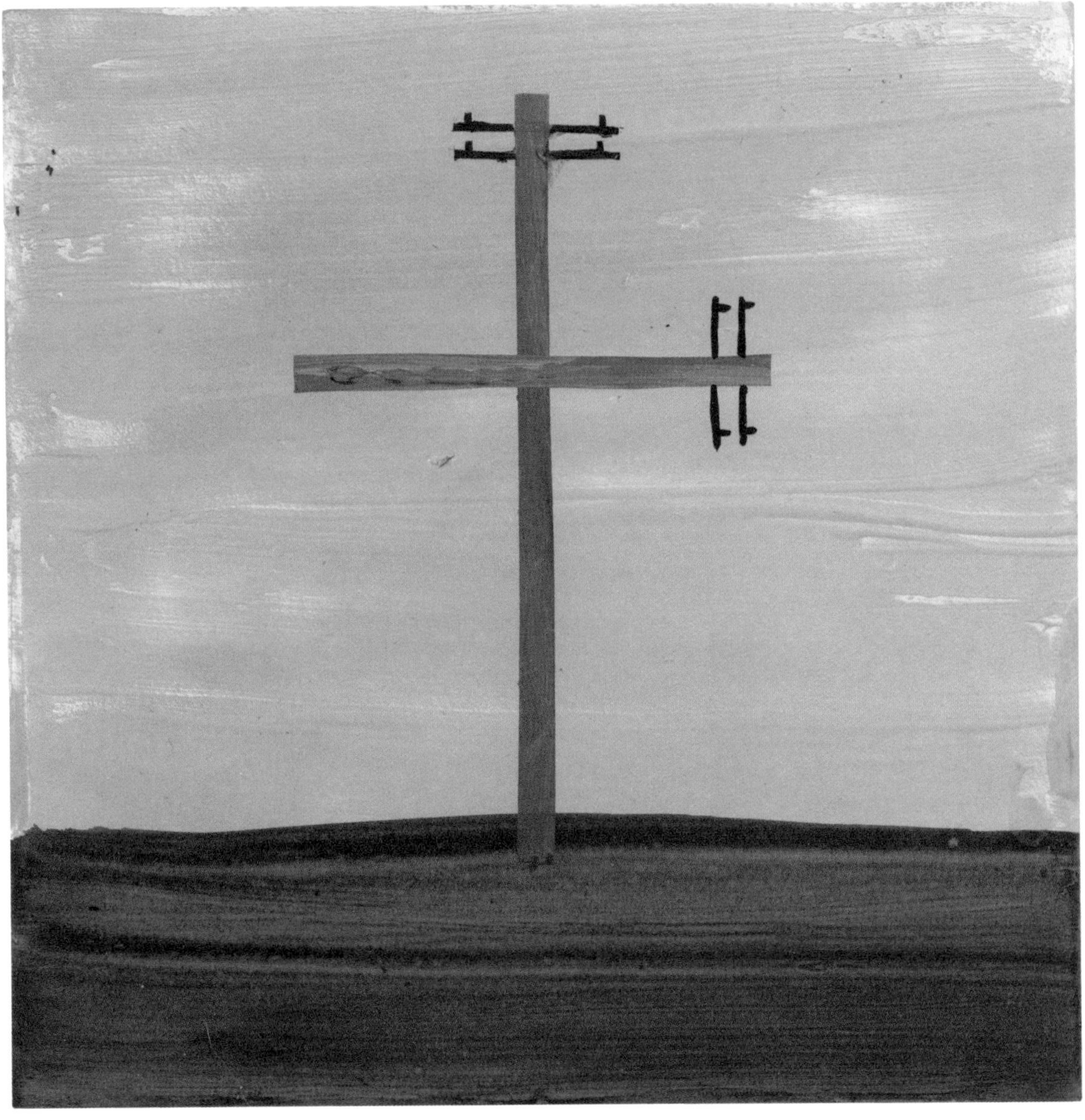

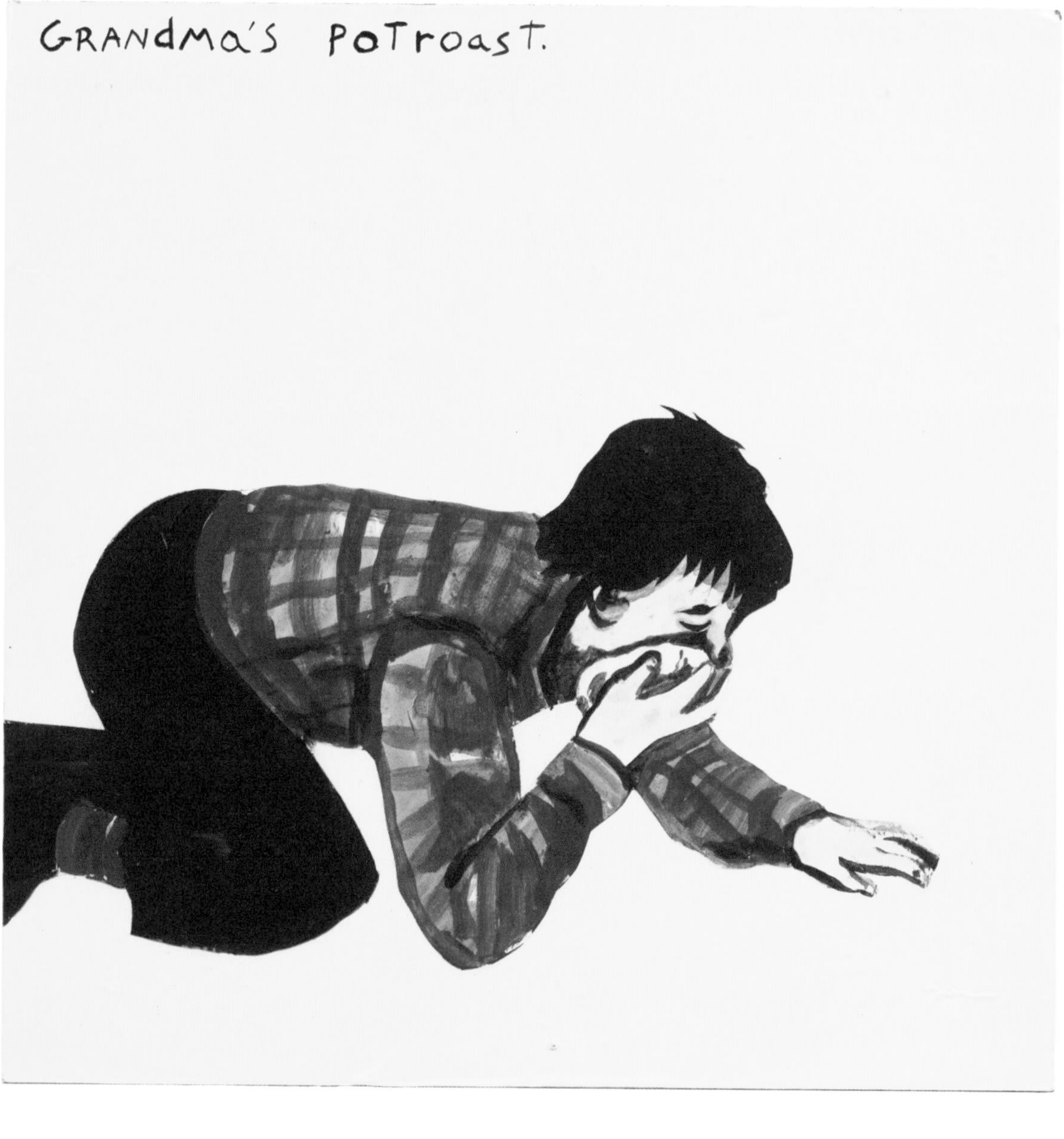
GRANDMA'S POTROAST.

HAPPY
40th
Birthday
Where ever
You live
love
Len
Jody
carly
TOM

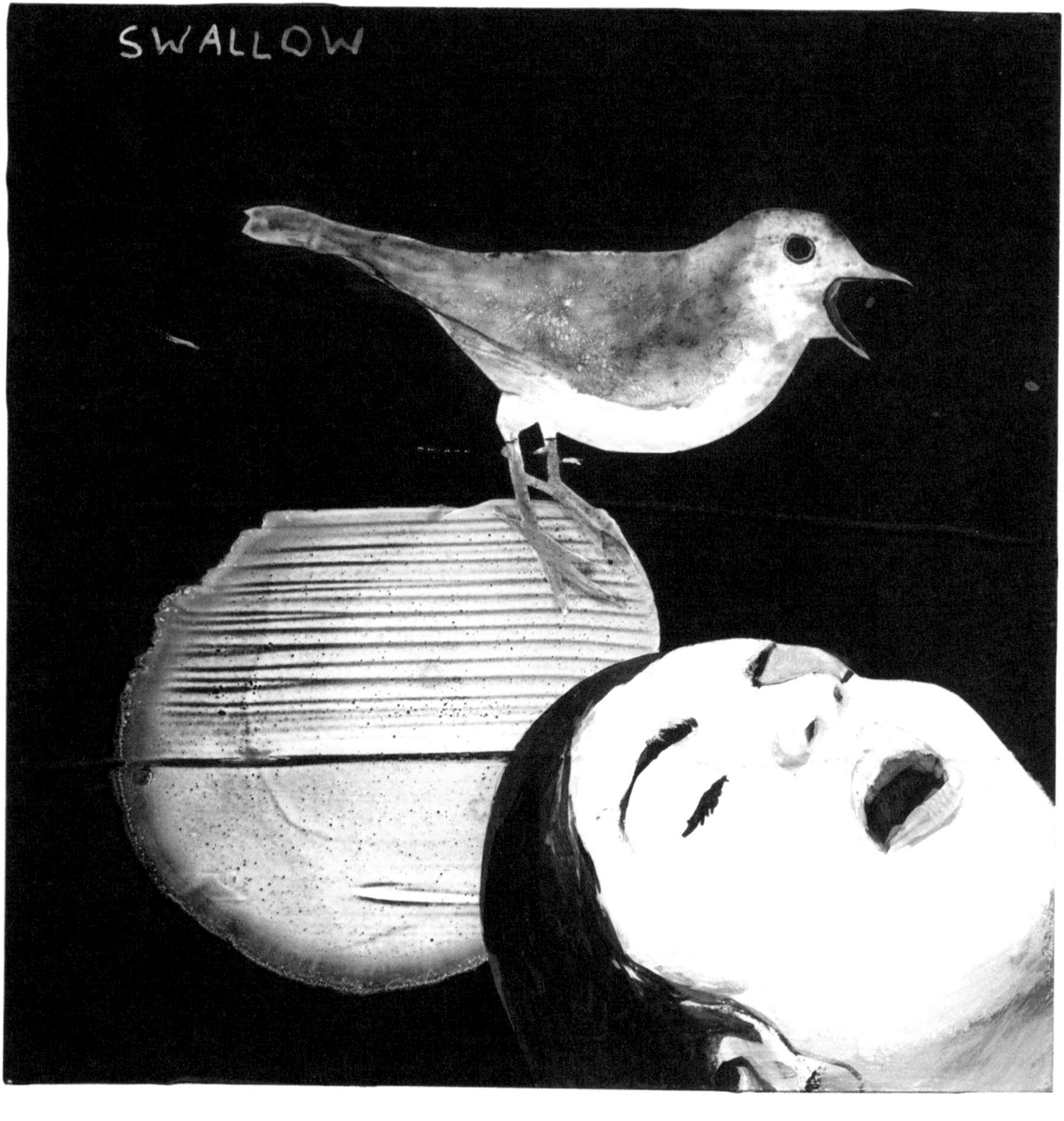
SWALLOW

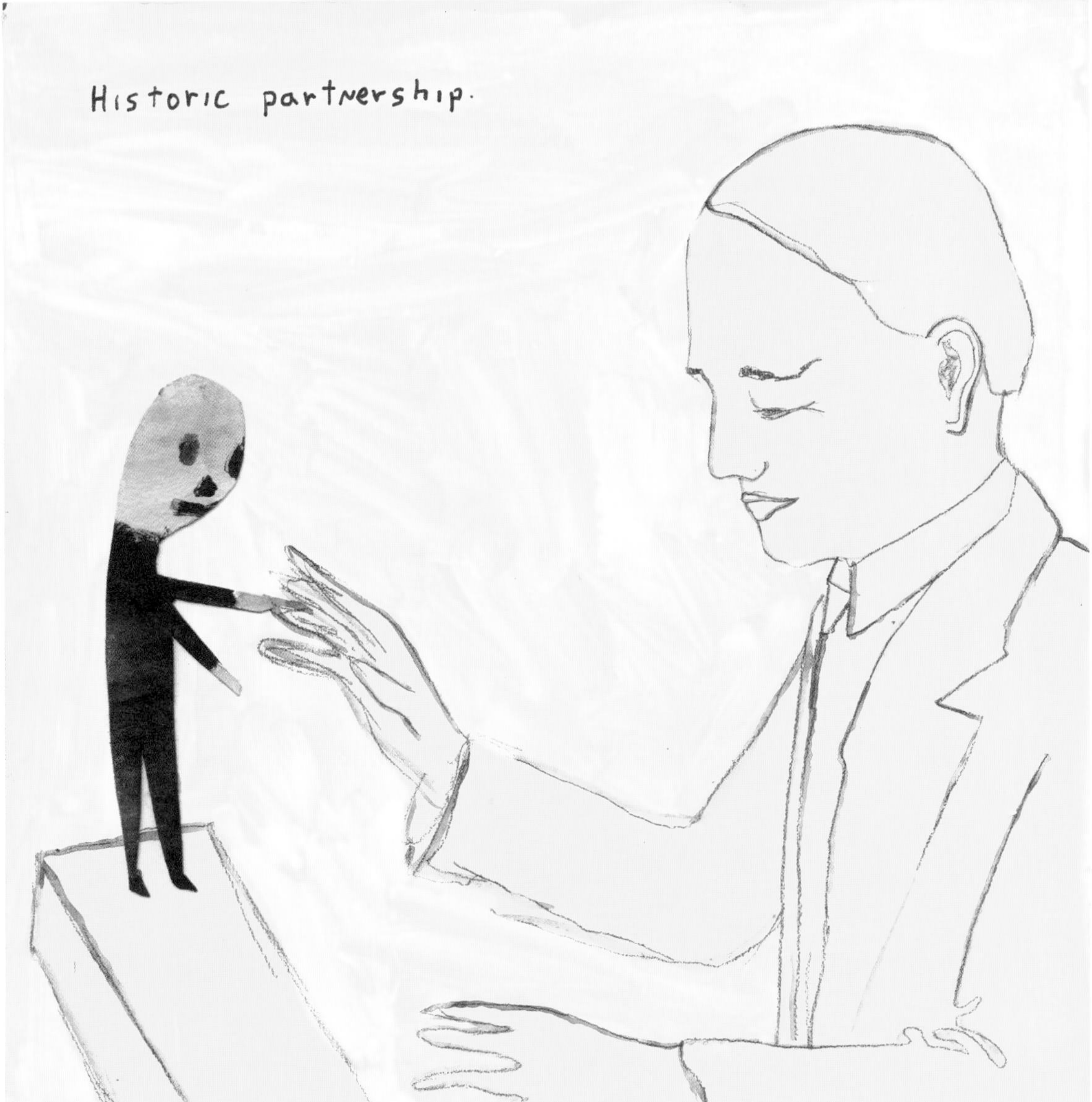
Historic partnership.

With fasting and jogging, you could hardly tell she was pregnant.

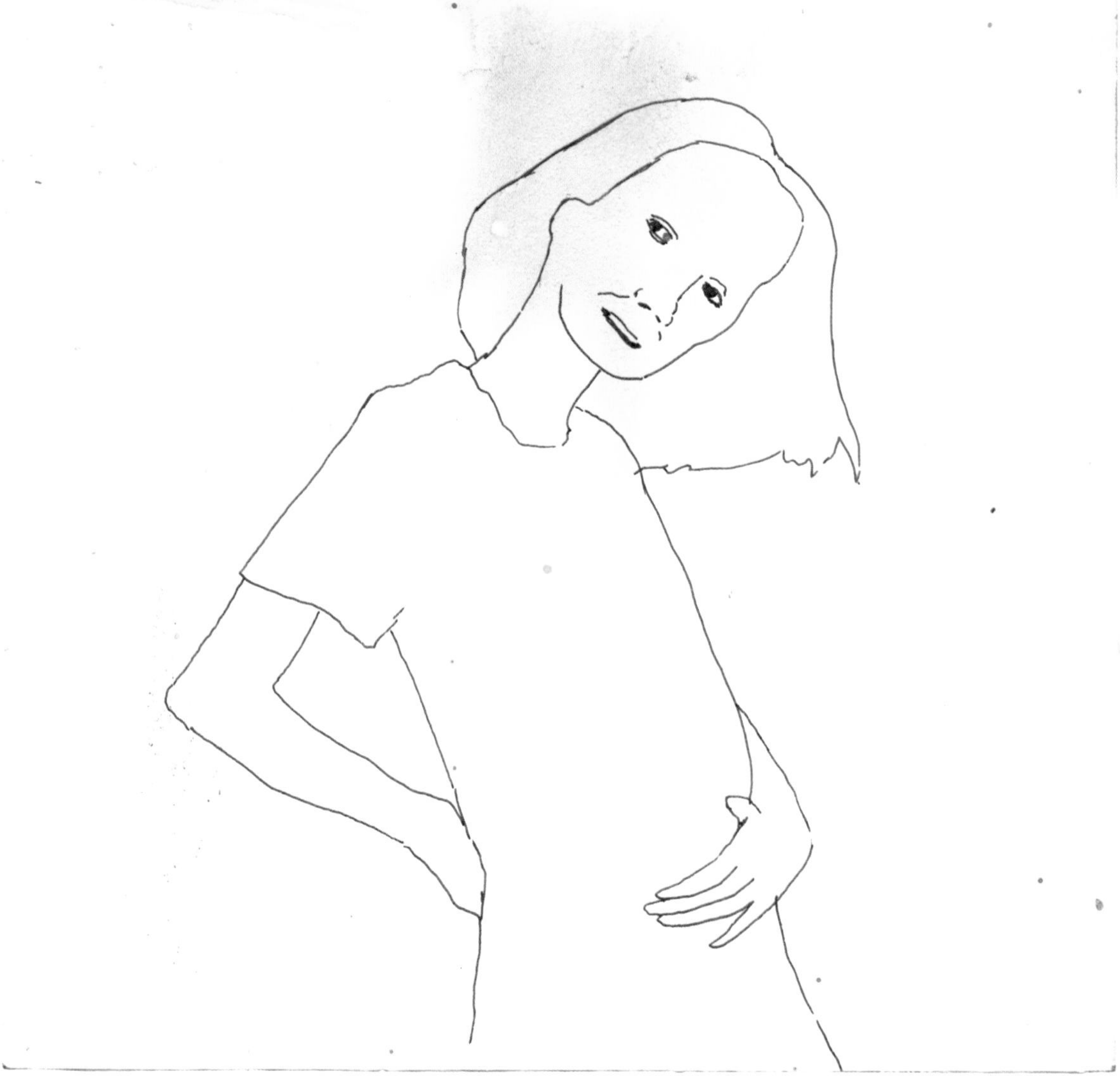

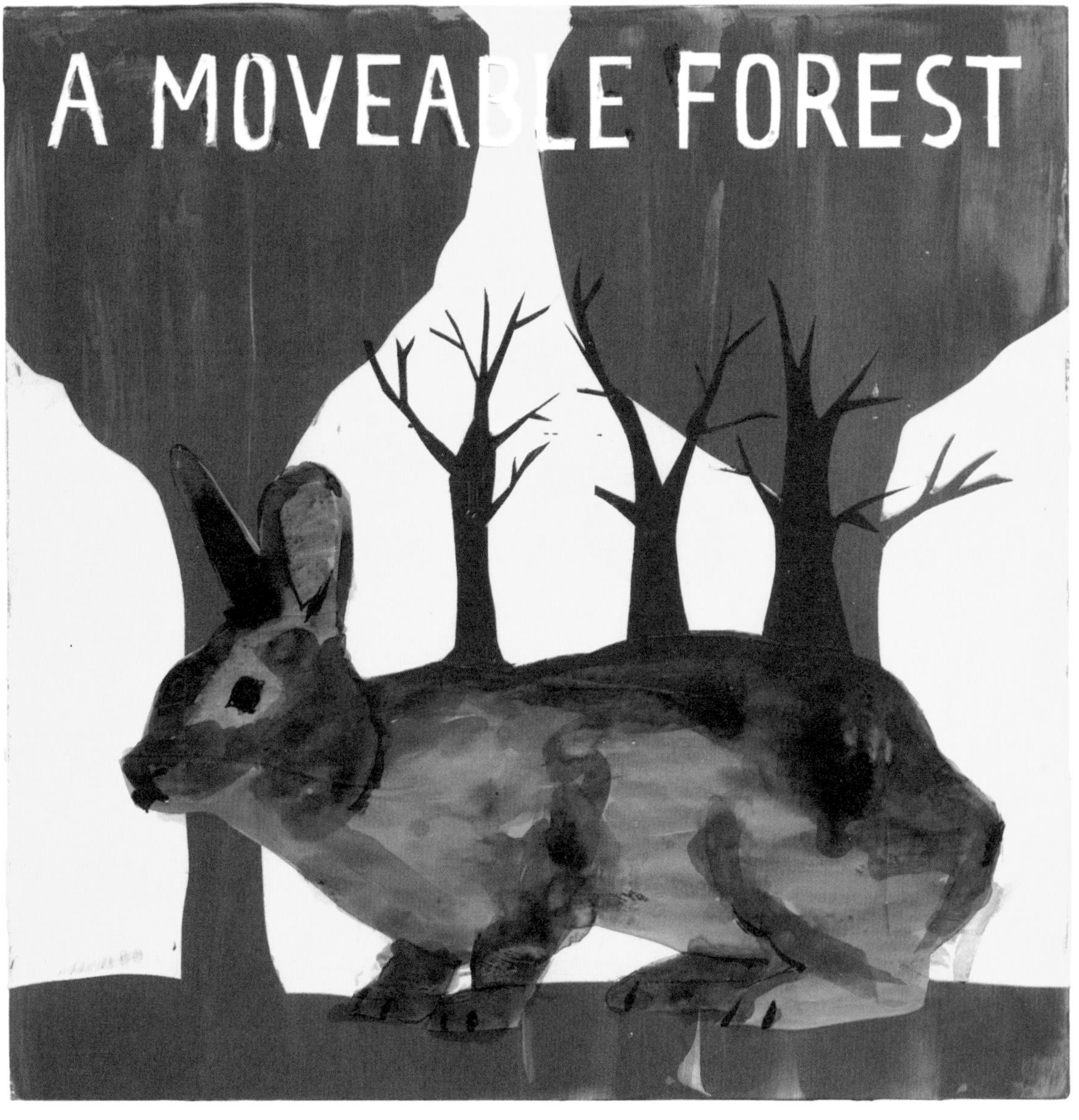
A MOVEABLE FOREST

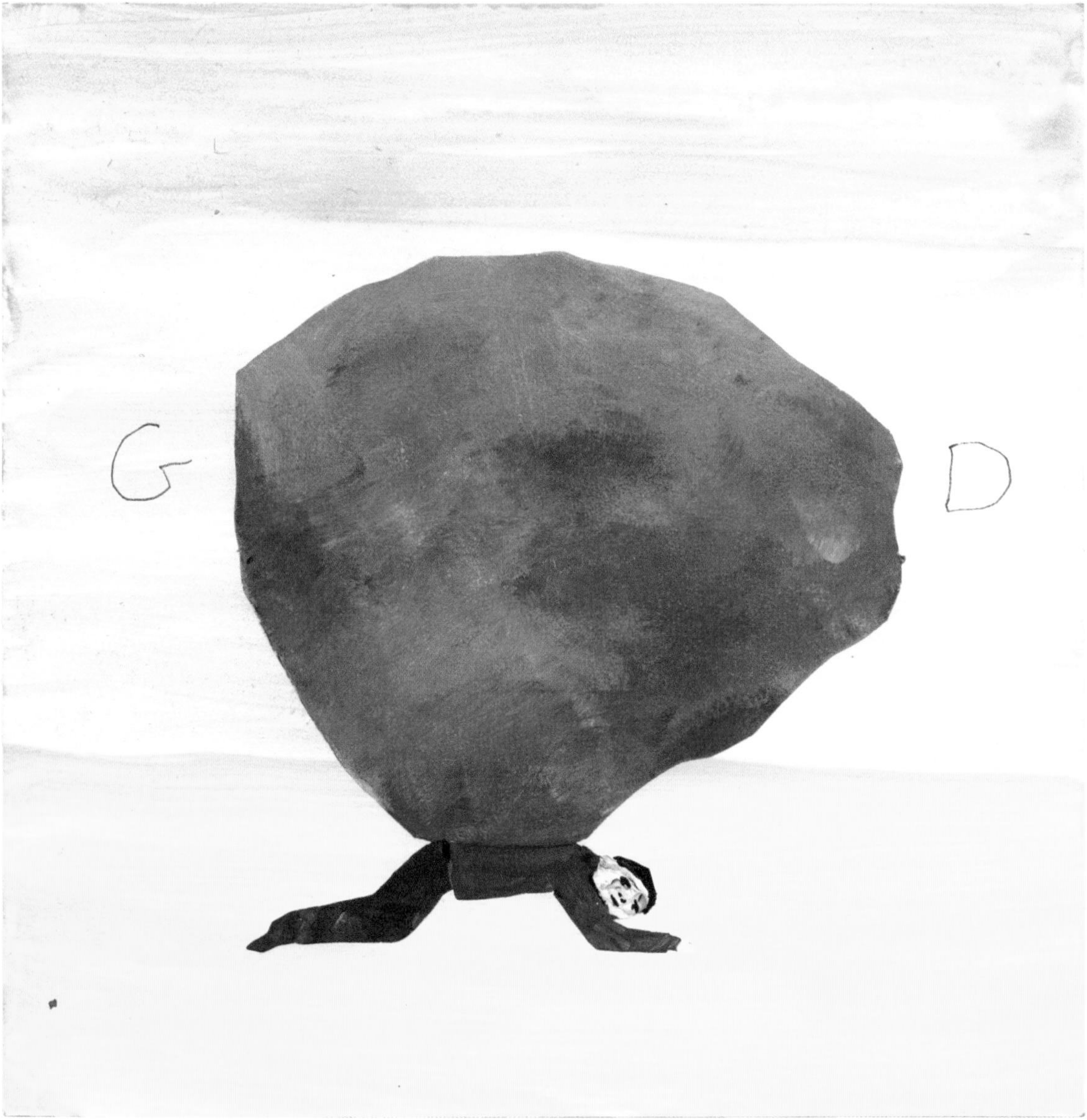
G D

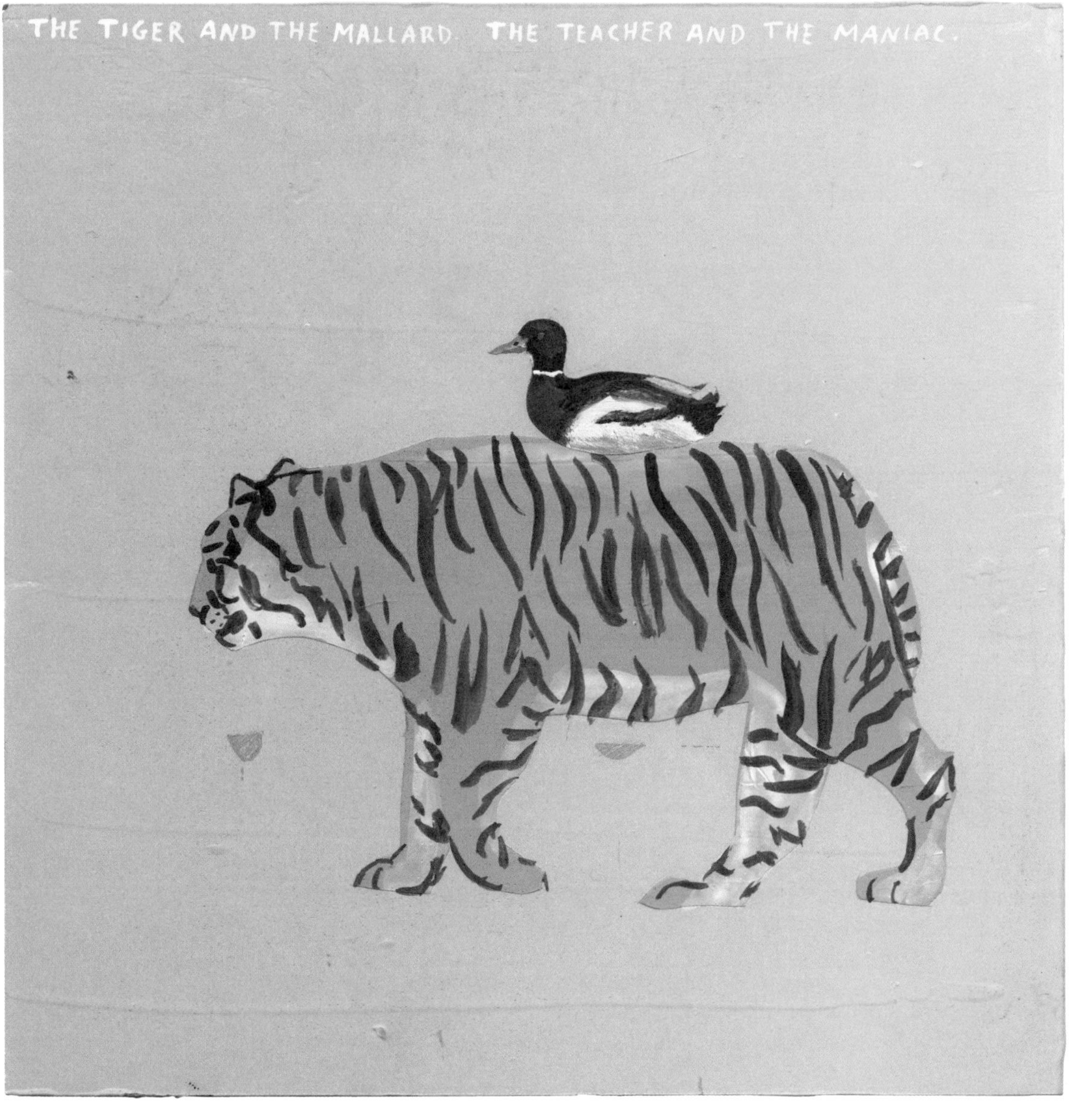
THE TIGER AND THE MALLARD. THE TEACHER AND THE MANIAC.

there is not a creature alive whose heart wouldn't be warmed by the attentions of a young woman.

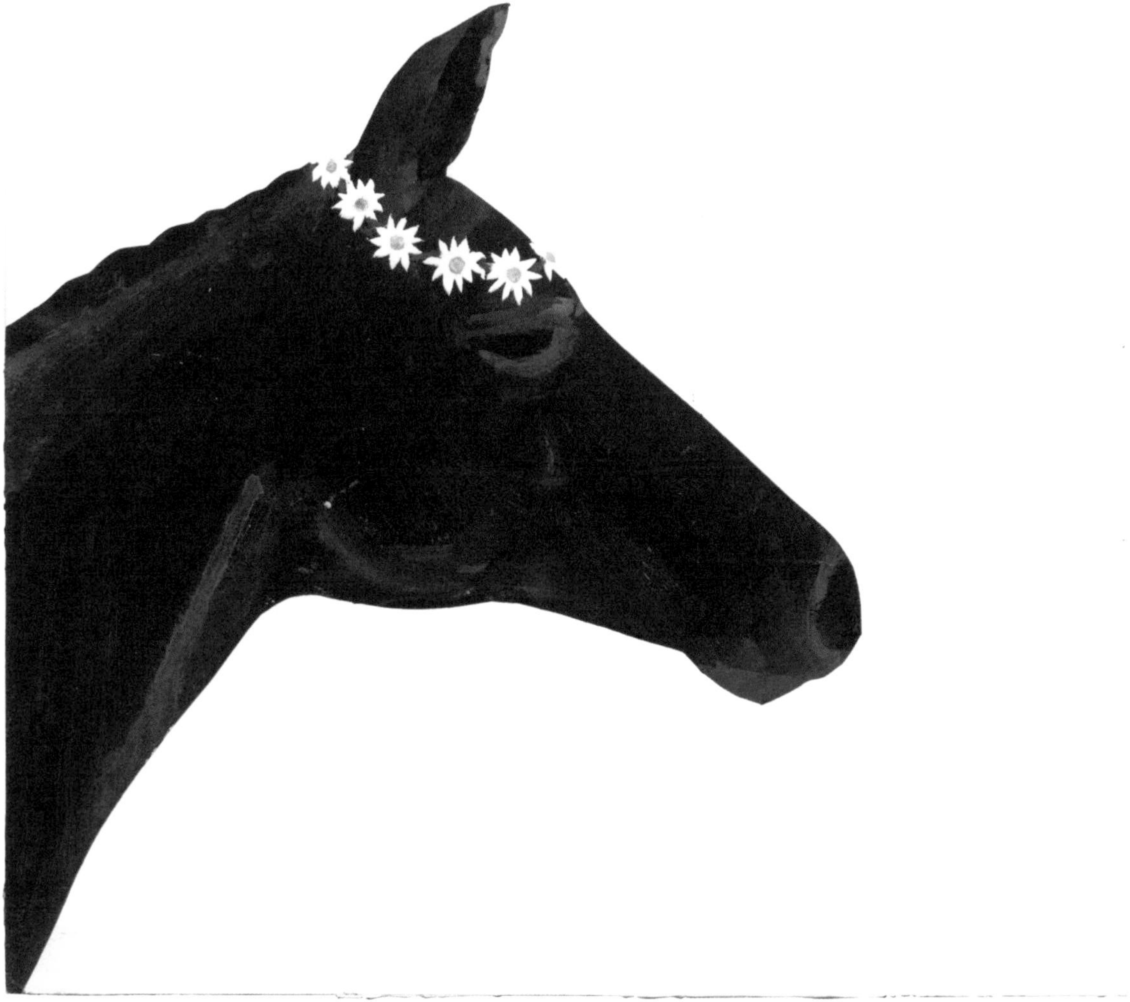

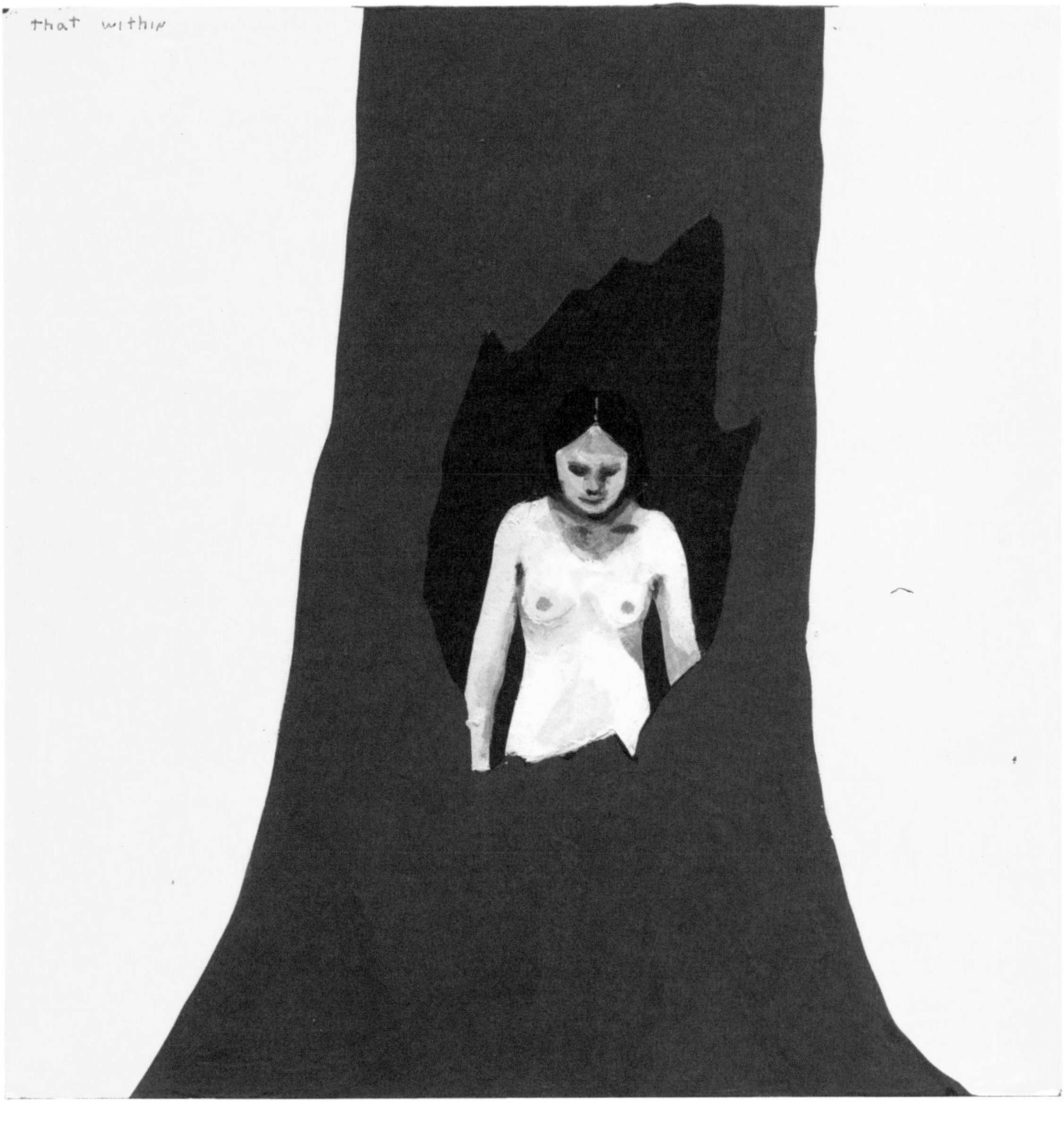
that within

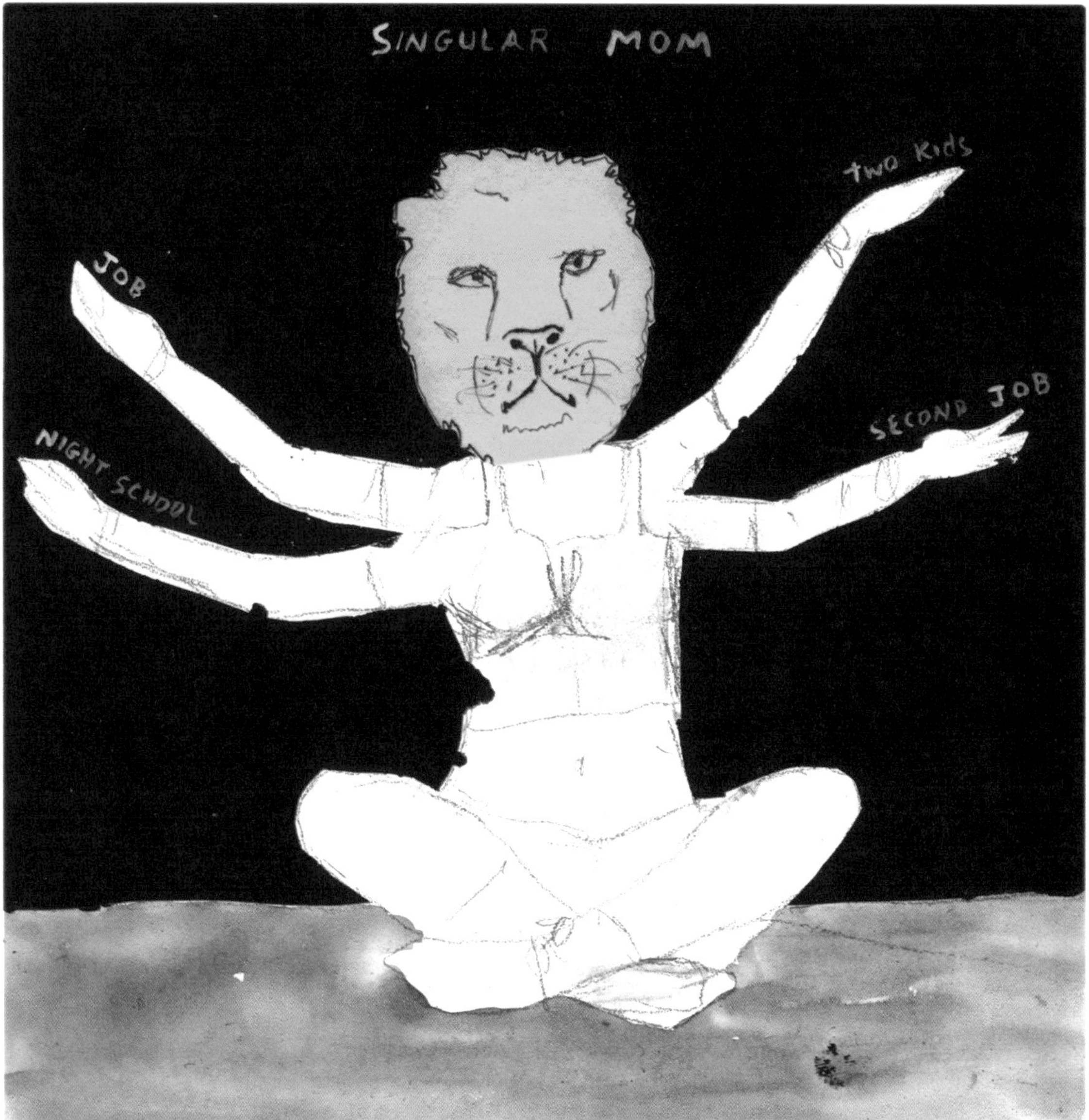
SINGULAR MOM
TWO KIDS
JOB
SECOND JOB
NIGHT SCHOOL

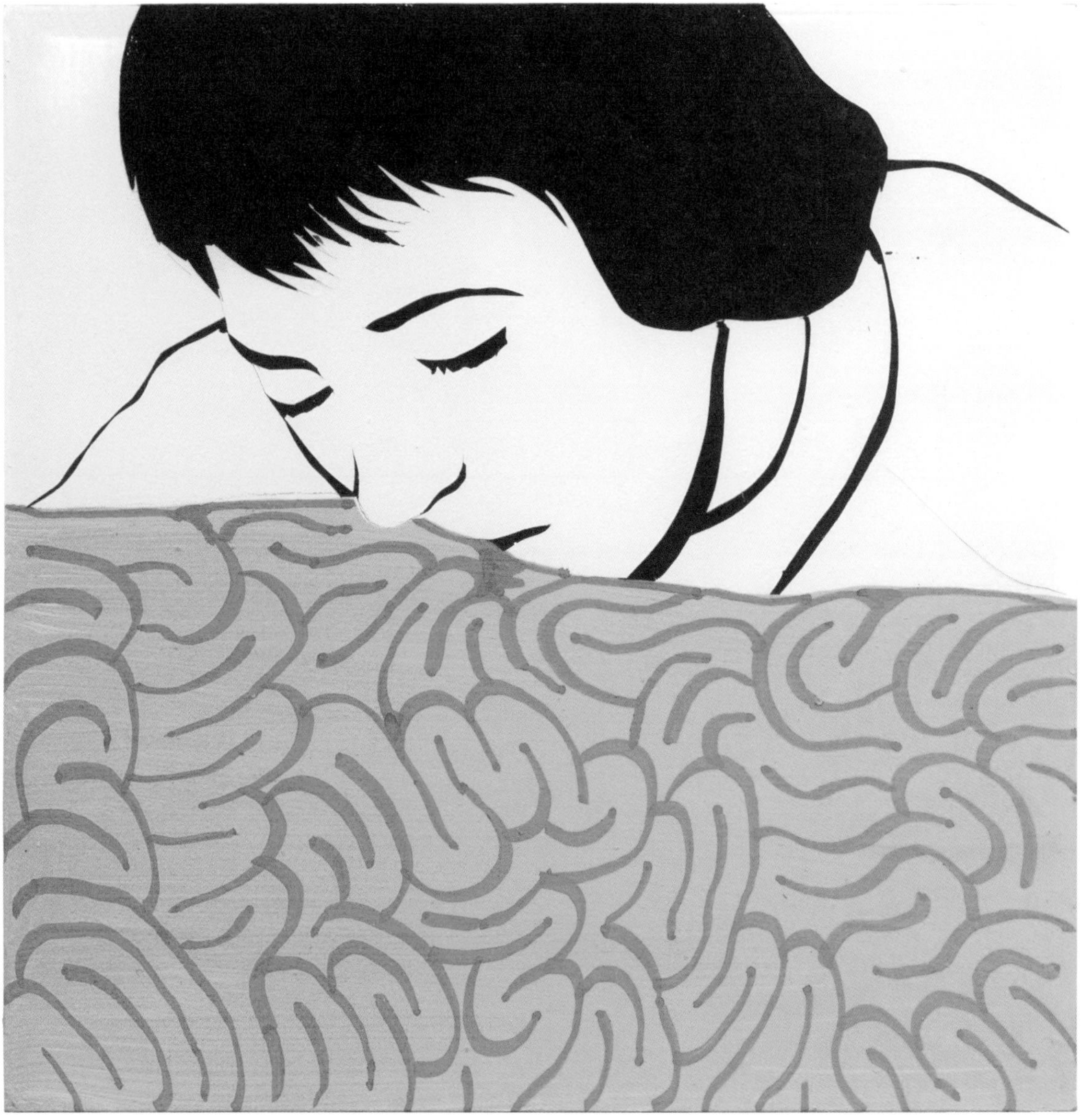

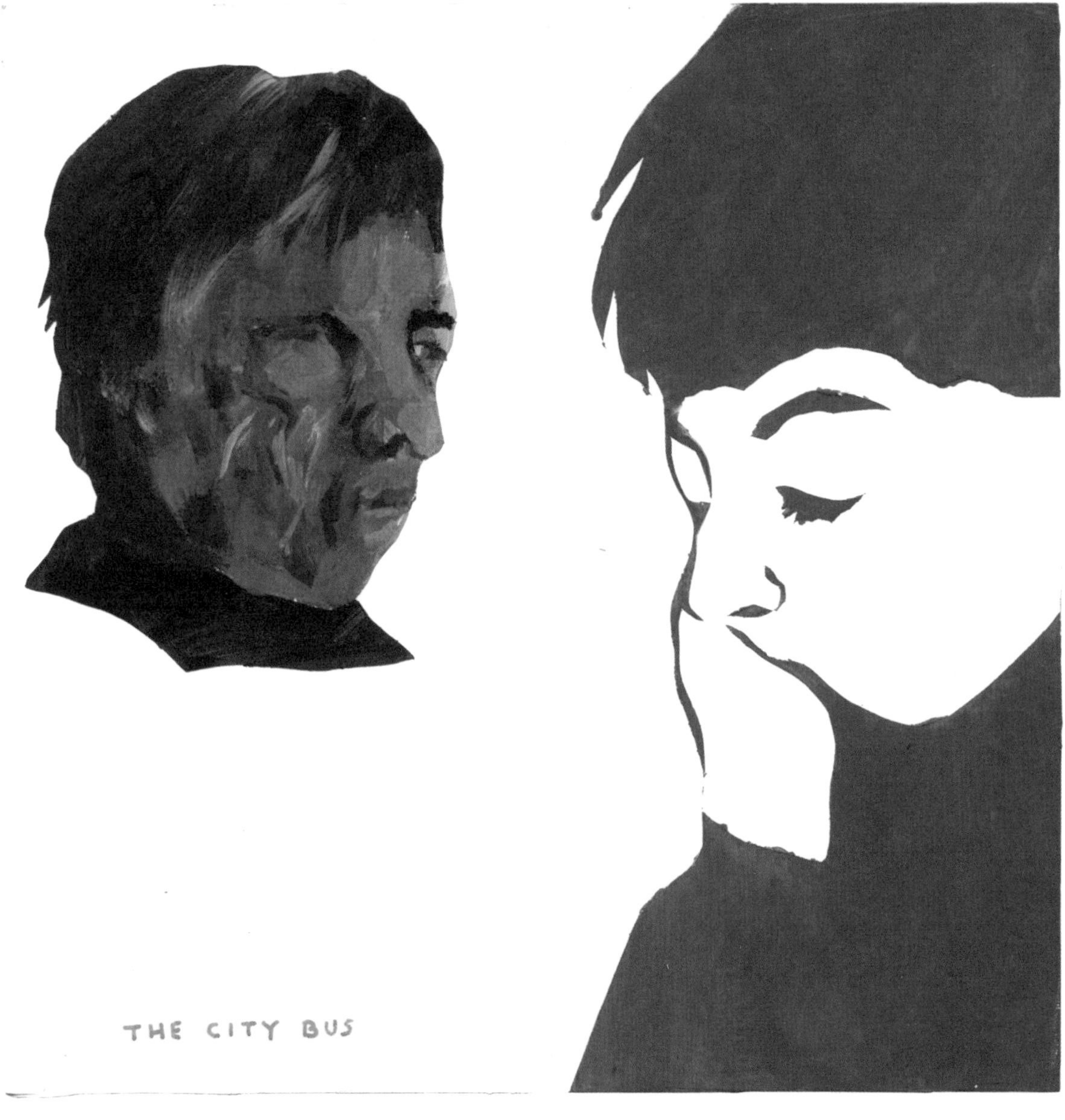
THE CITY BUS

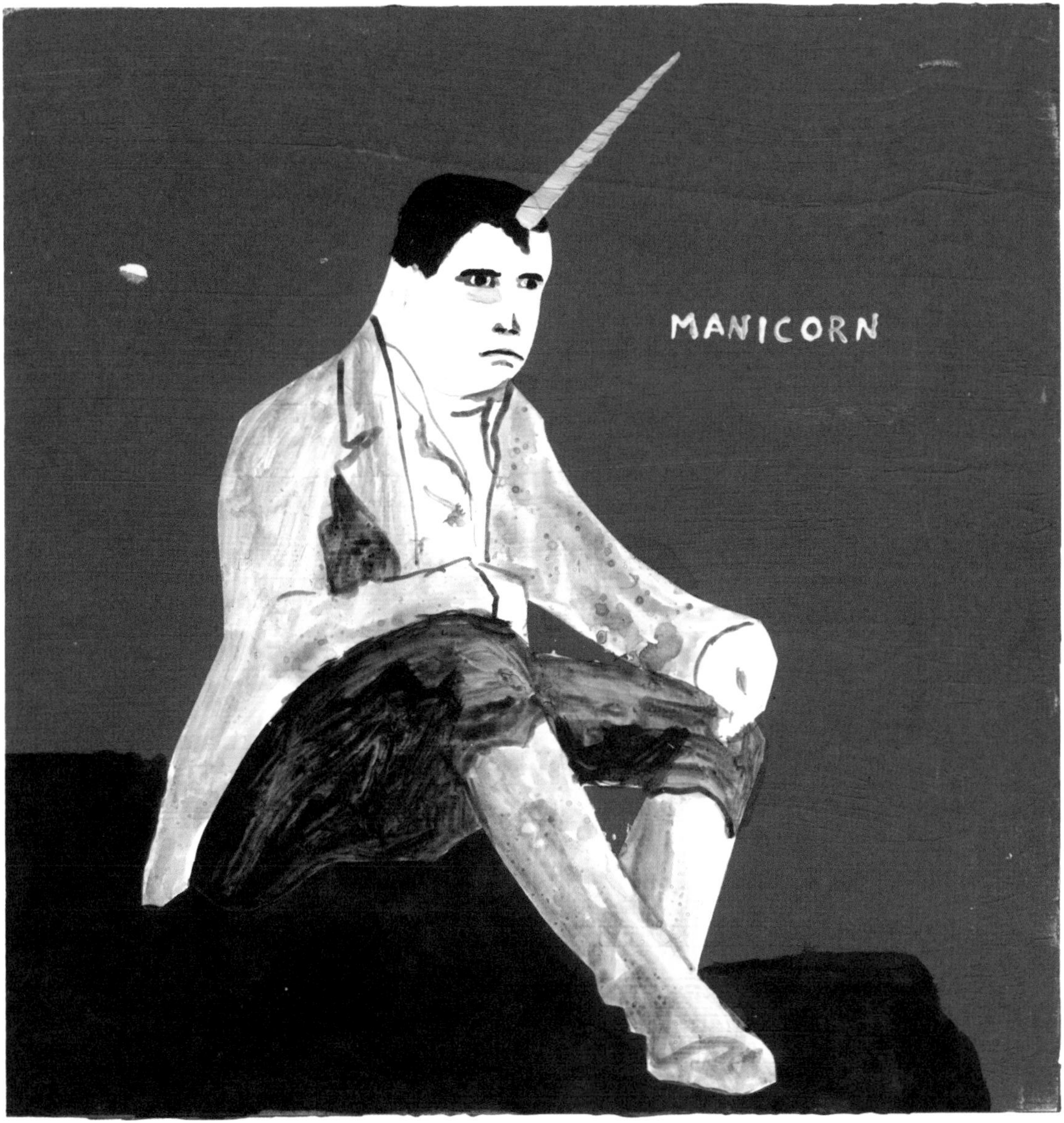
MANICORN

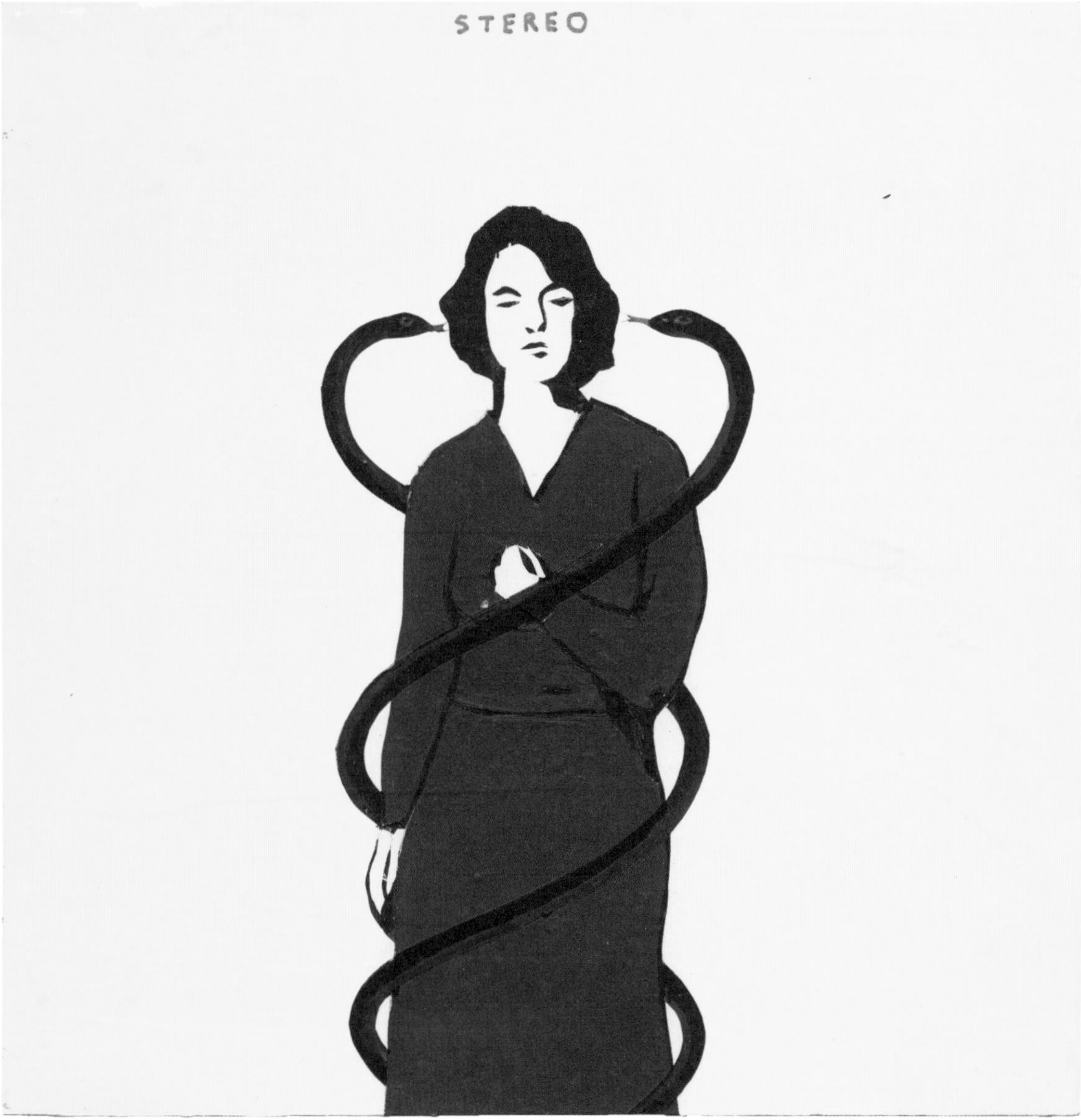
STEREO

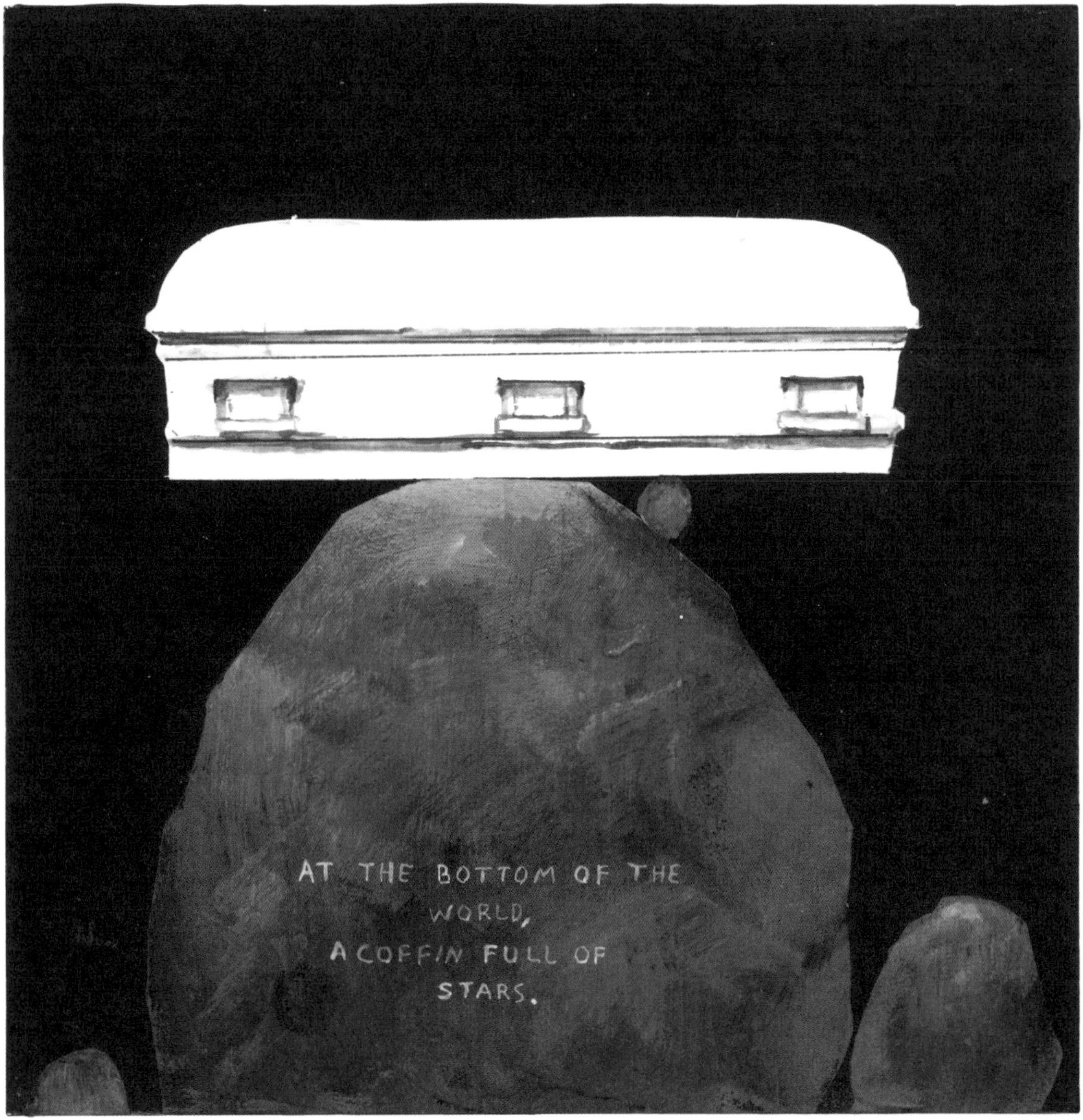
AT THE BOTTOM OF THE
WORLD,
A COFFIN FULL OF
STARS.

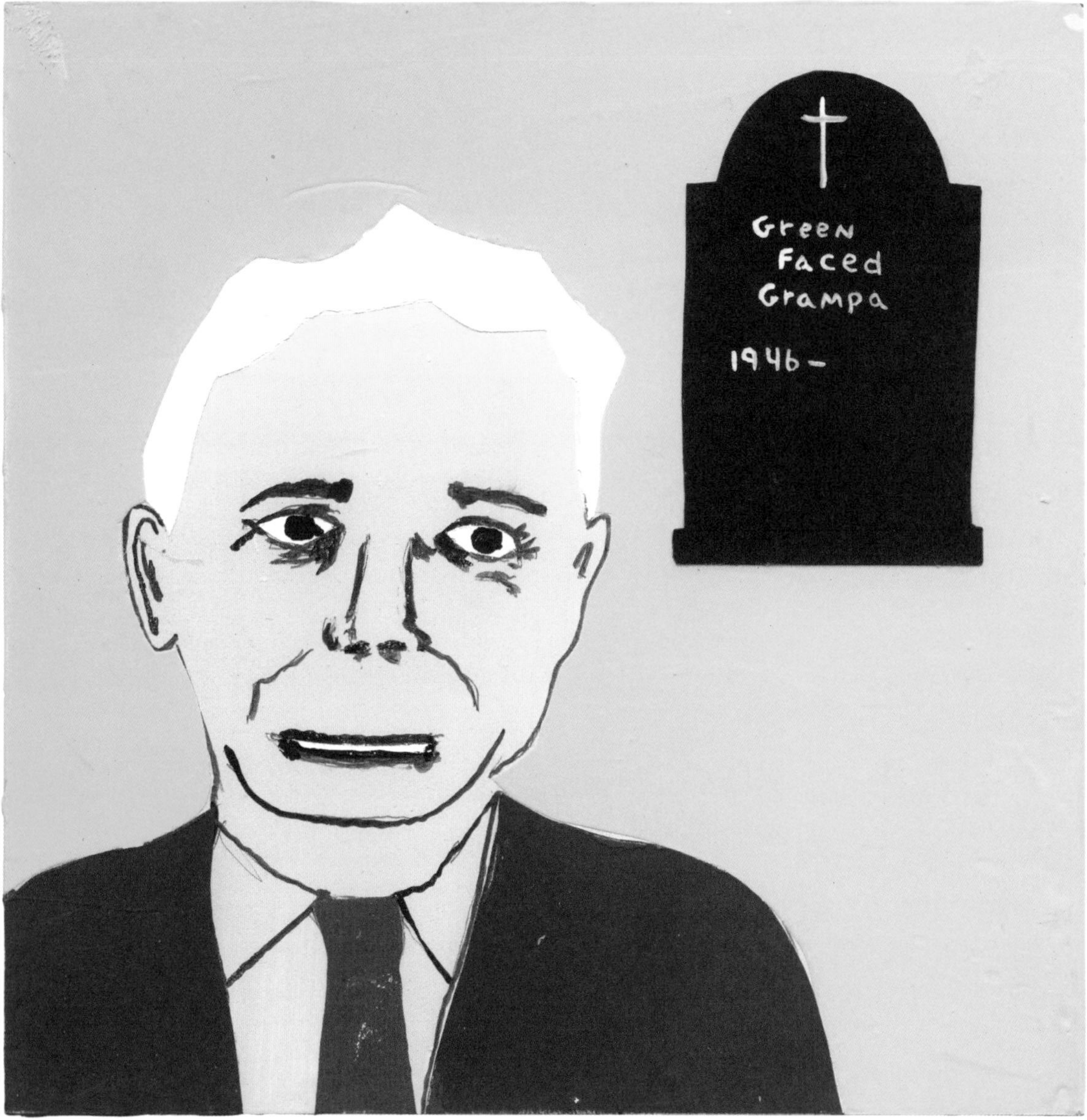
Green
Faced
Grampa
1946–

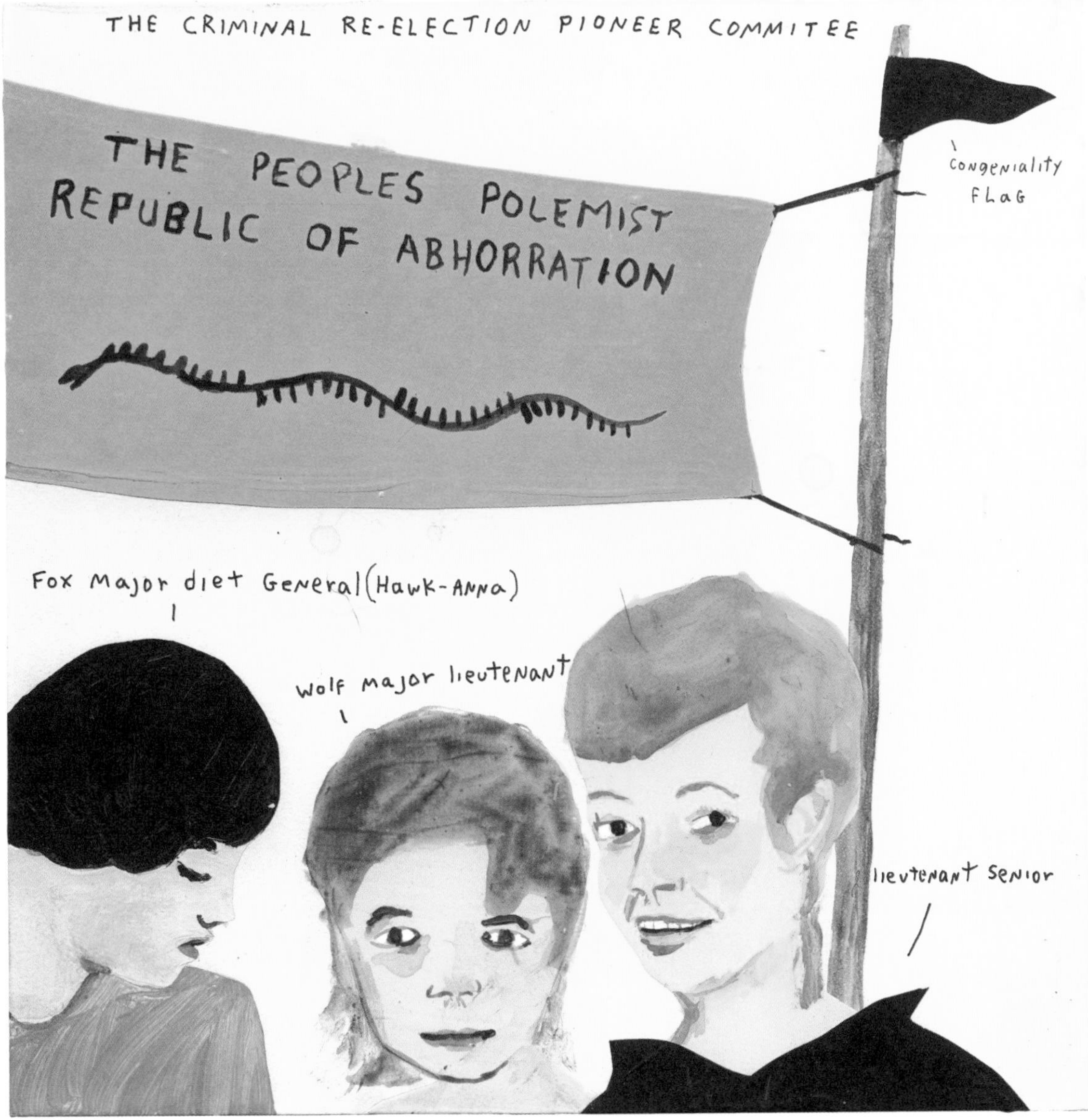
THE CRIMINAL RE-ELECTION PIONEER COMMITEE
THE PEOPLES POLEMIST REPUBLIC OF ABHORRATION
congeniality flag
Fox major diet General (Hawk-Anna)
wolf major lieutenant
lieutenant senior

Recital

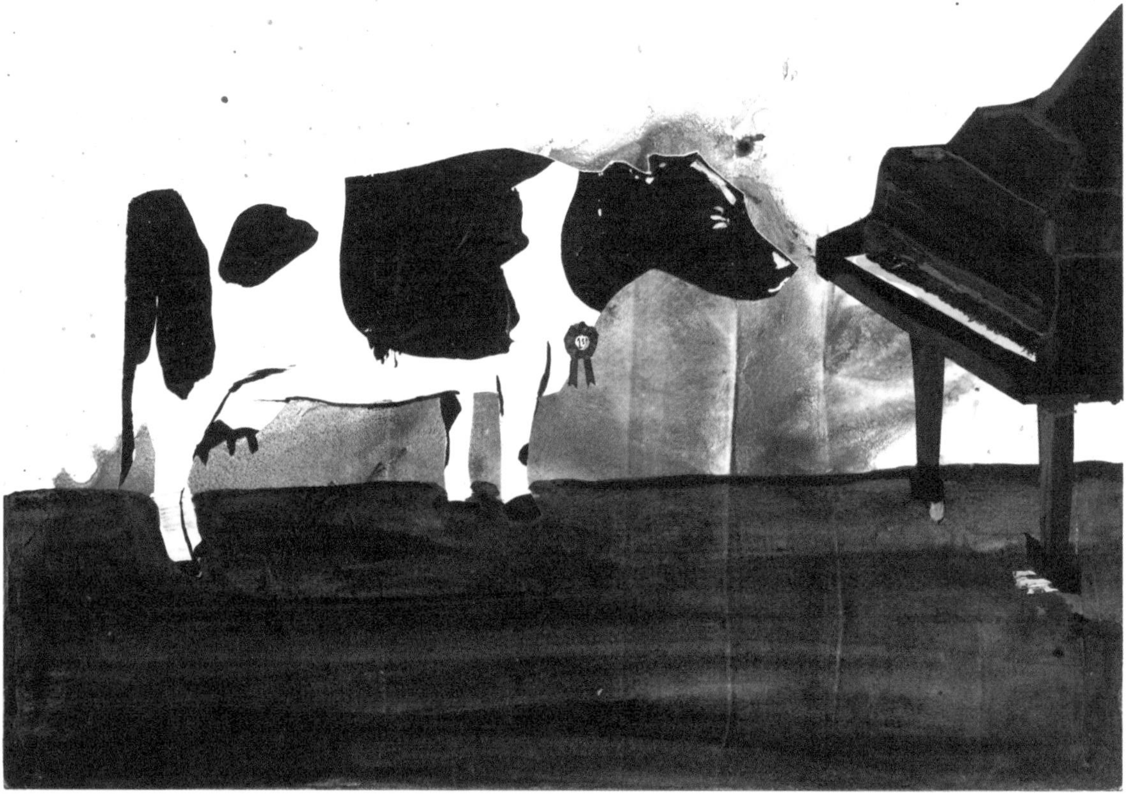

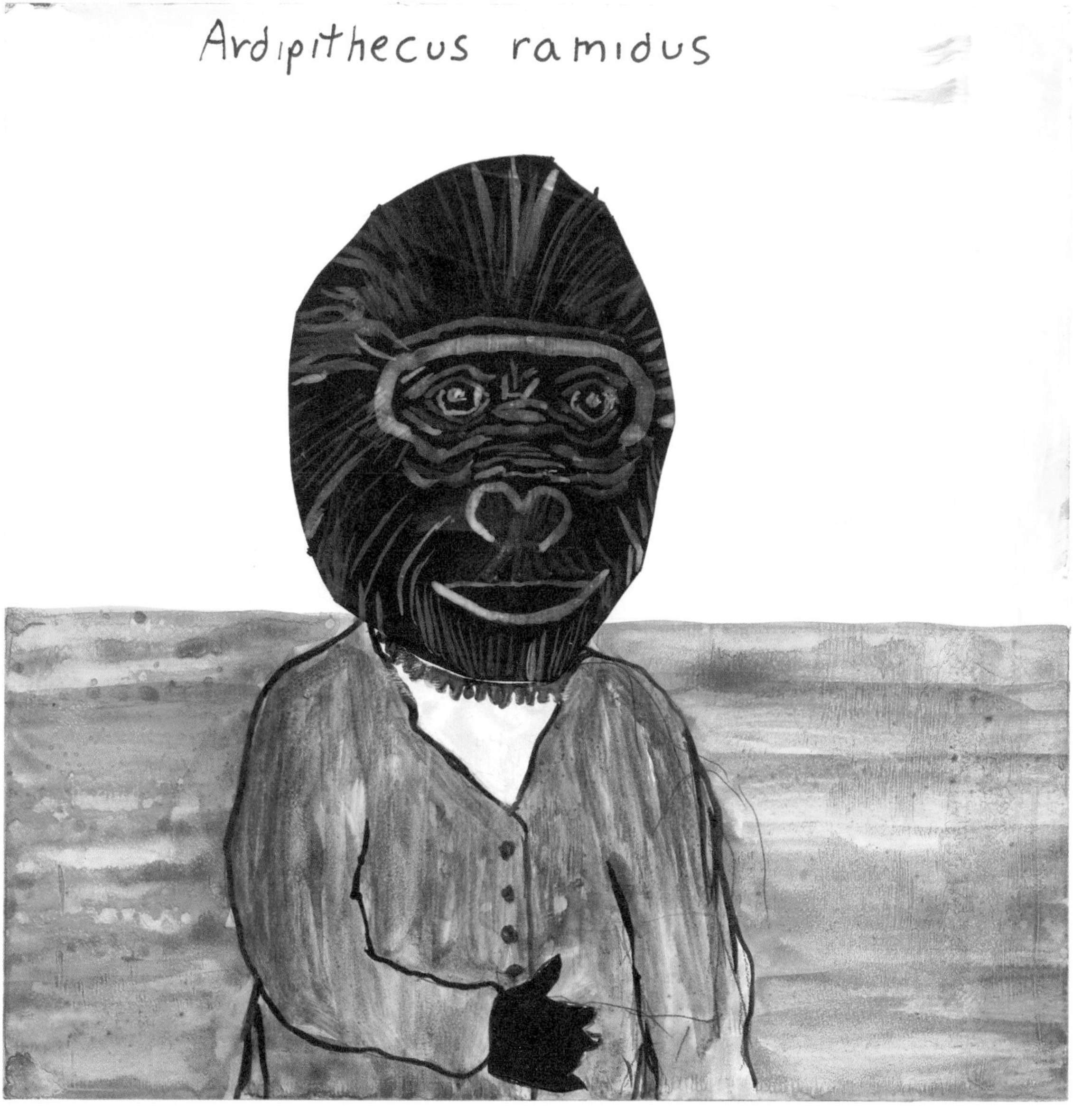
Ardipithecus ramidus

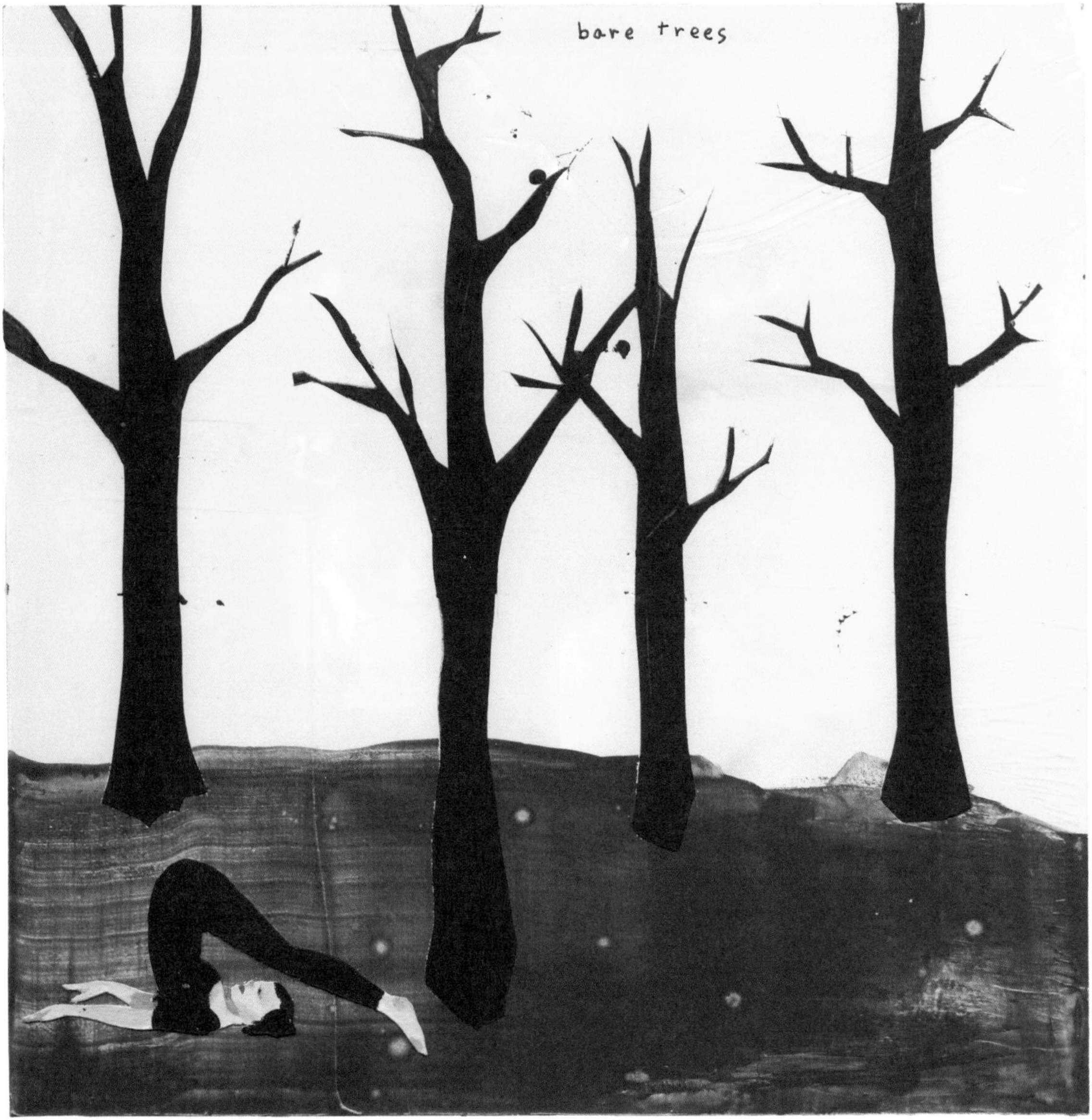
bare trees

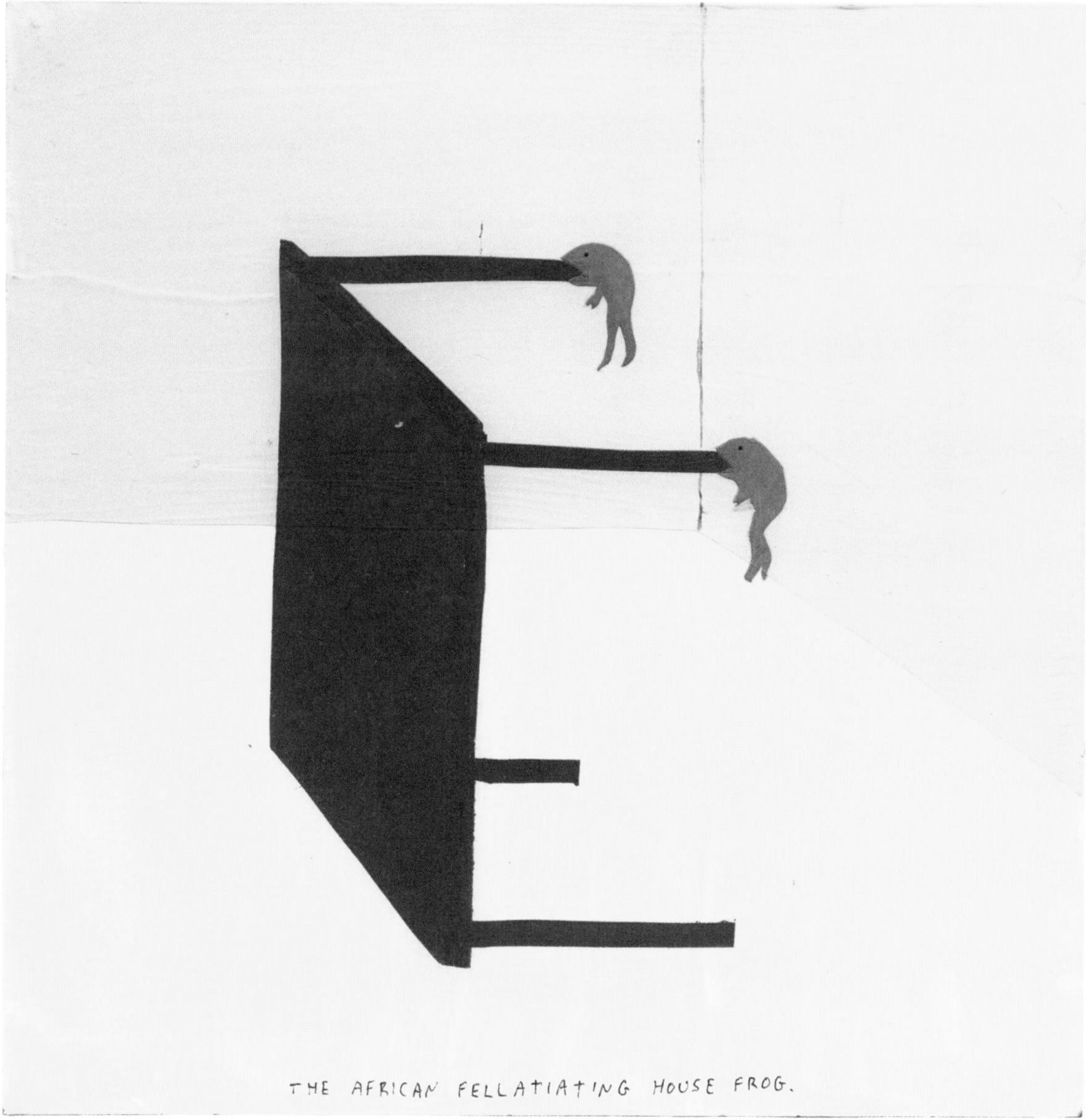

THE AFRICAN FELLATIATING HOUSE FROG.

I STARTLED HIM, AND HE FAINTED, but
I think he is O.K. What ARE YOU
GOING to do with HIM? I'LL probably
go over to the dam and show him to
beaver and then leave him over by
the big tree. Sounds good. I'll come
with. I haven't seen Beaver in a
long time.

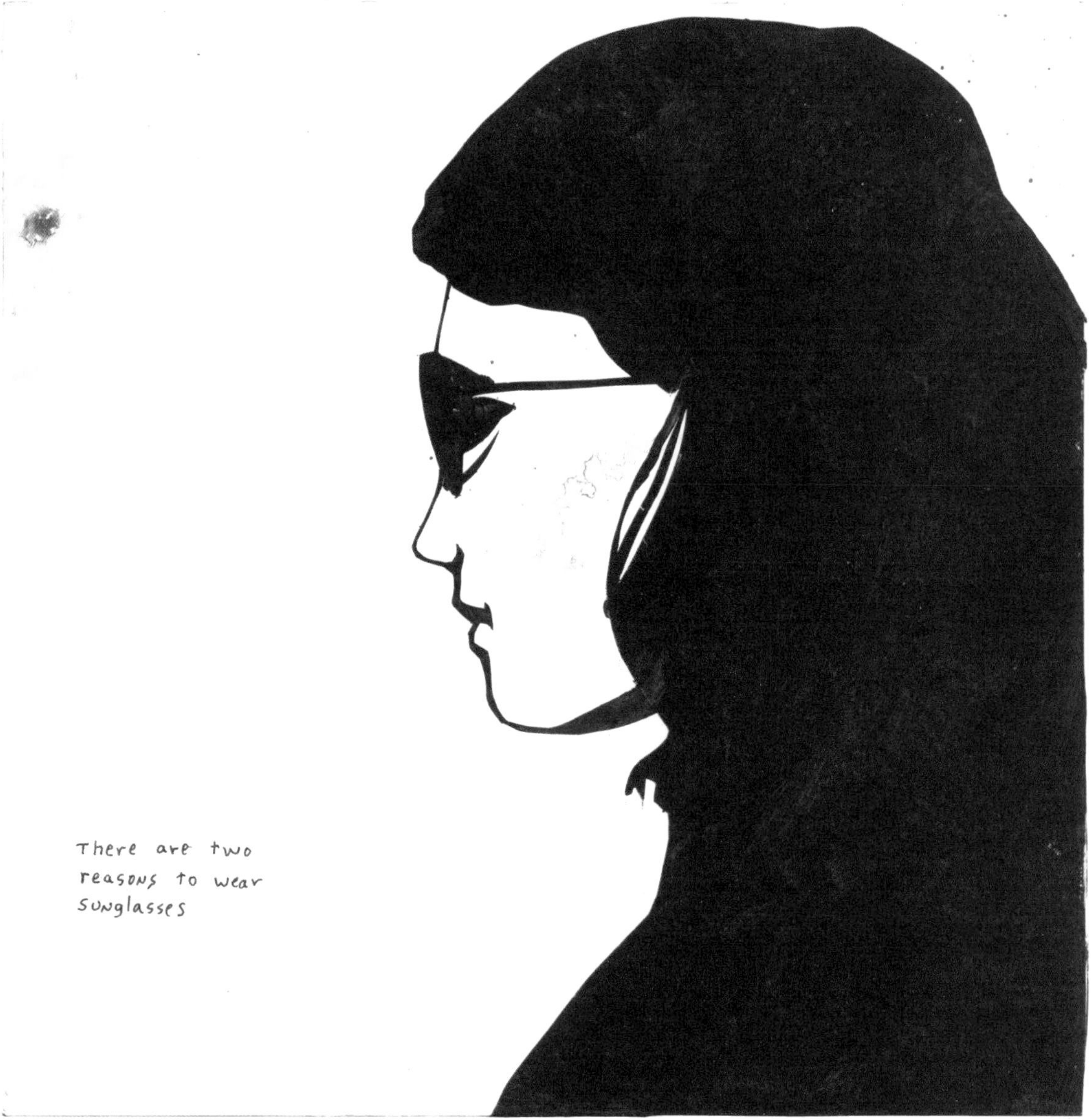
There are two
reasons to wear
sunglasses

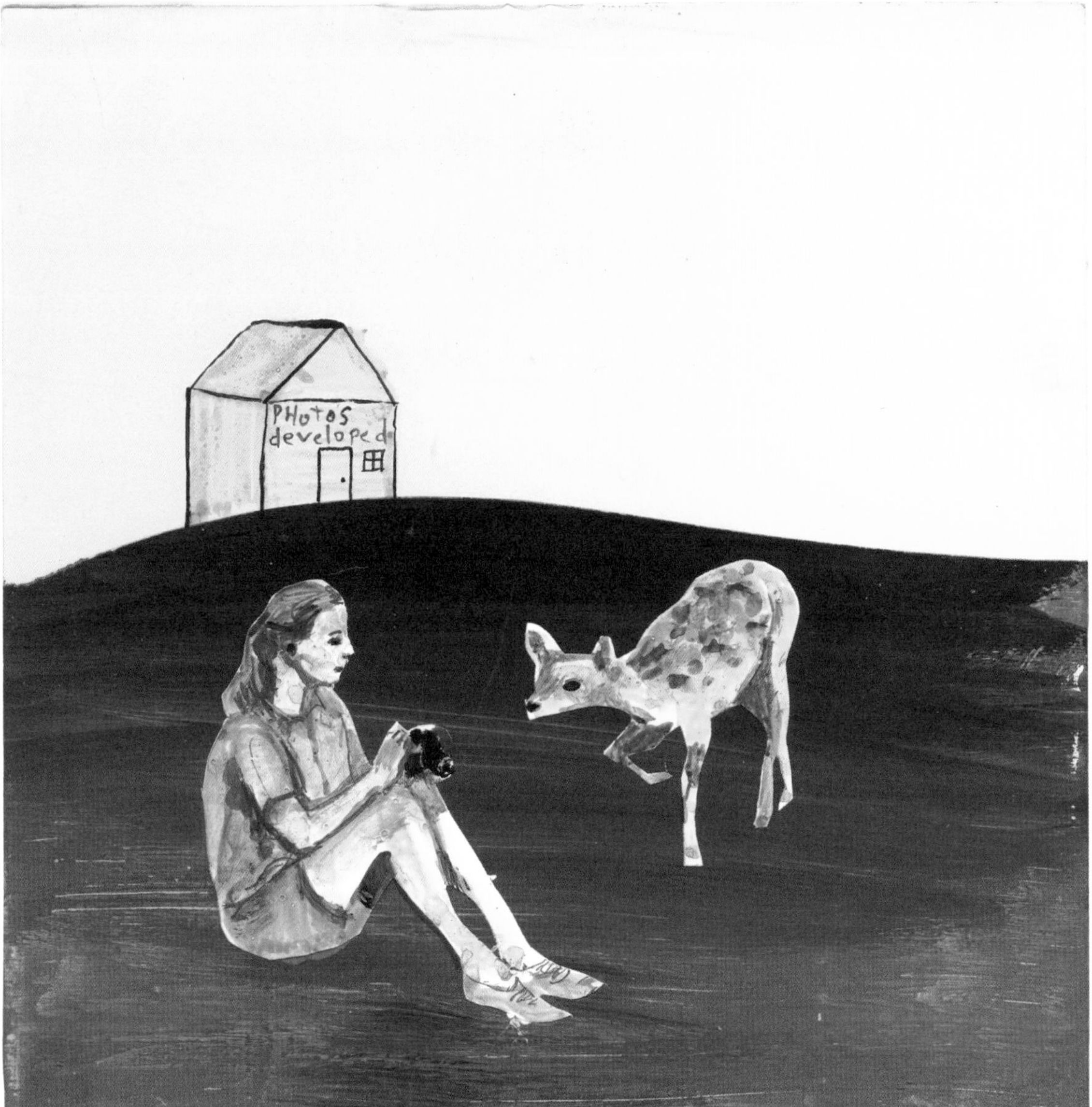
PHOTOS
developed

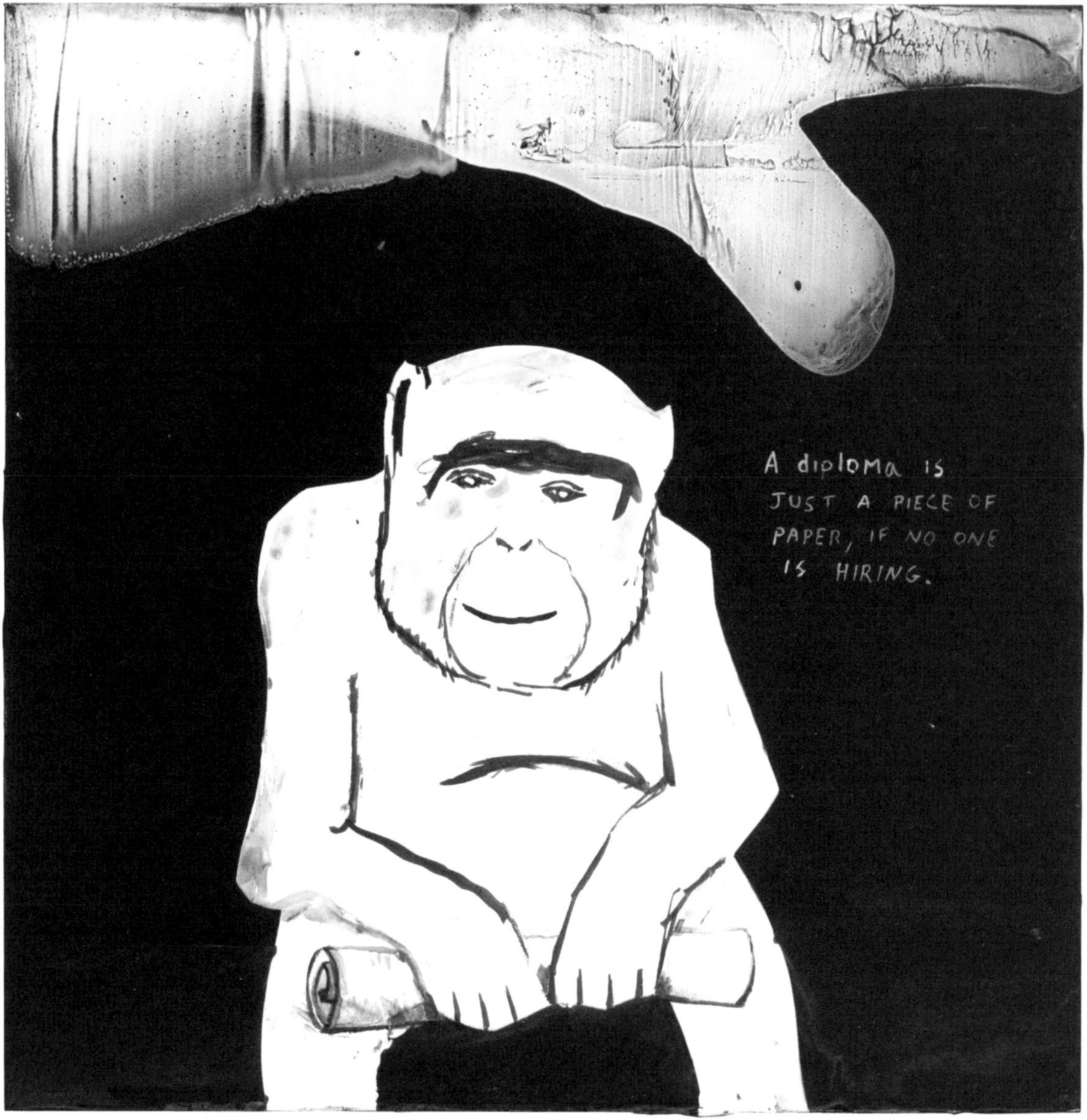
A diploma is
JUST A PIECE OF
PAPER, IF NO ONE
IS HIRING.

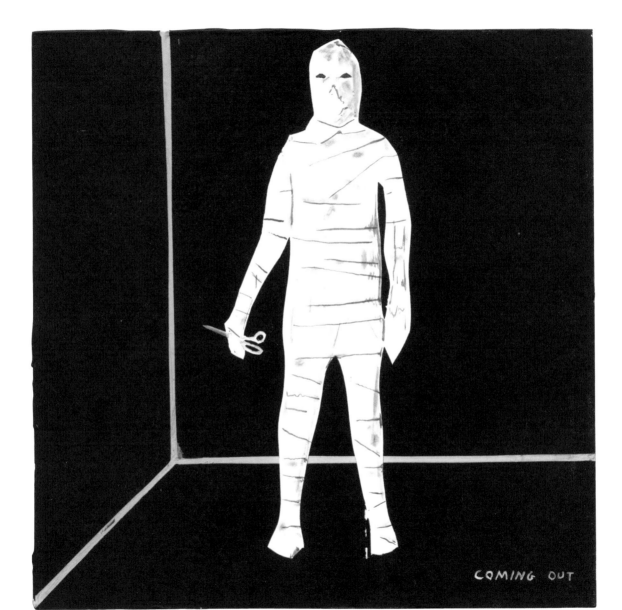

COMING OUT

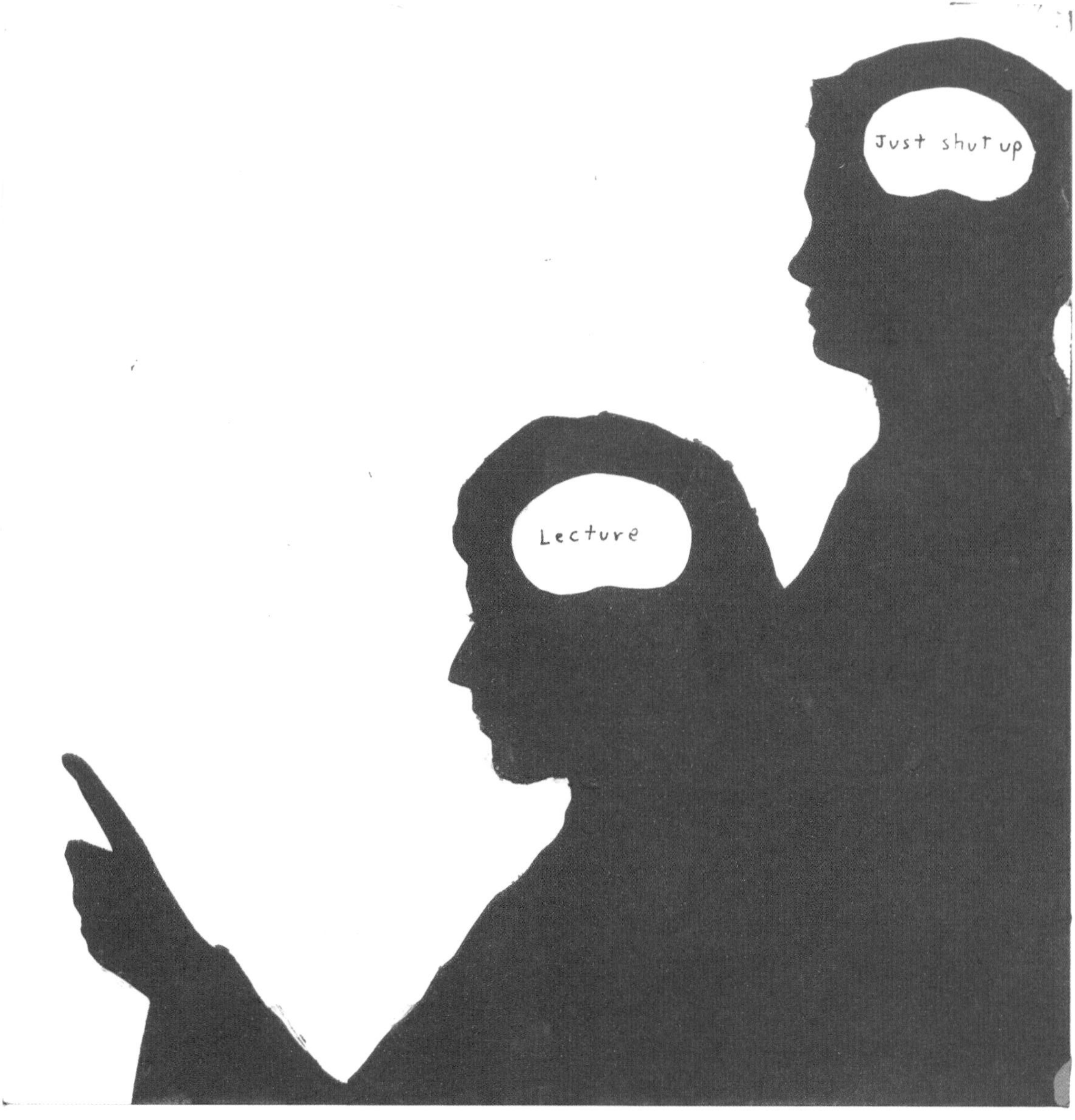
Just shut up
Lecture

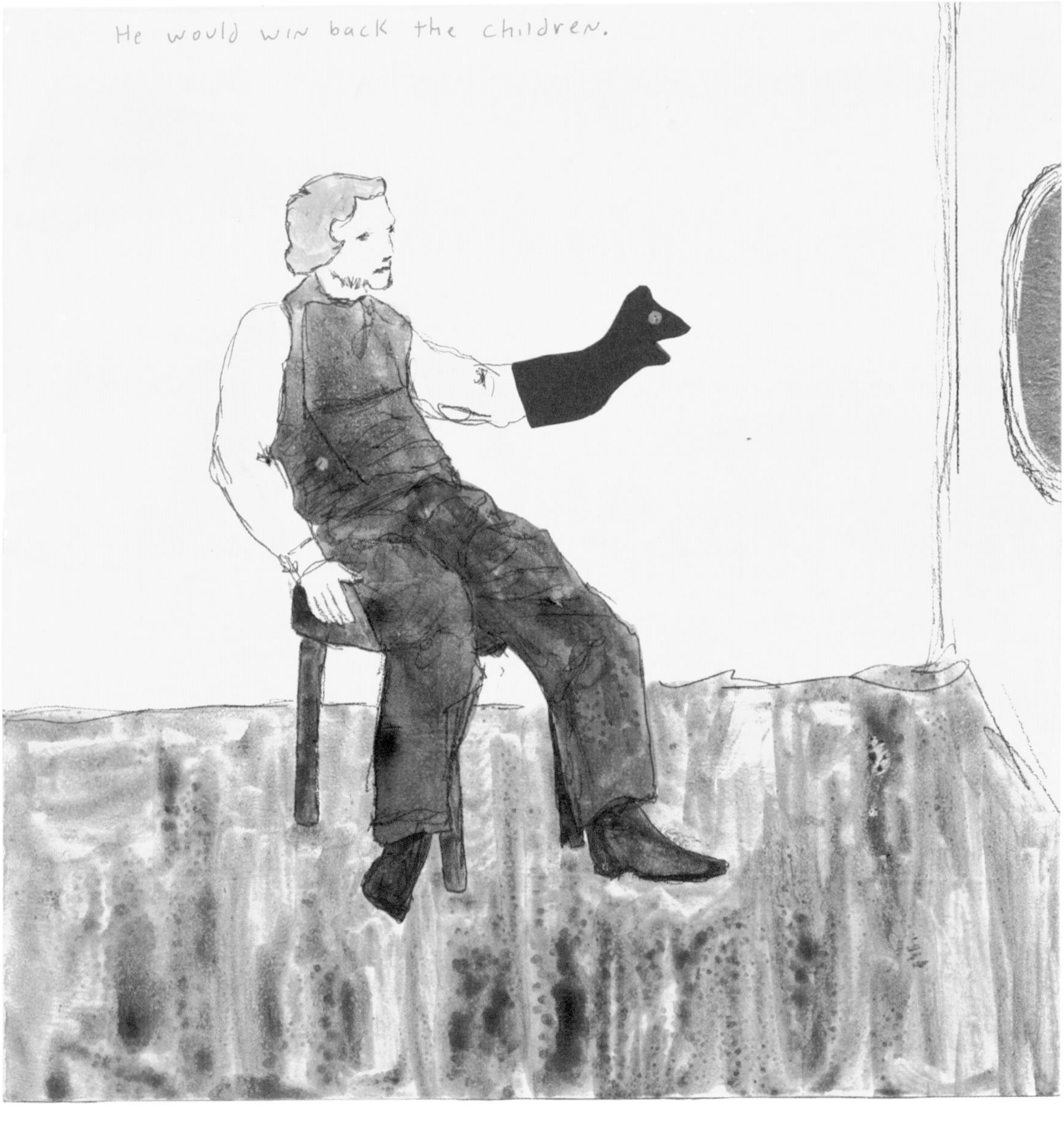
He would win back the children.

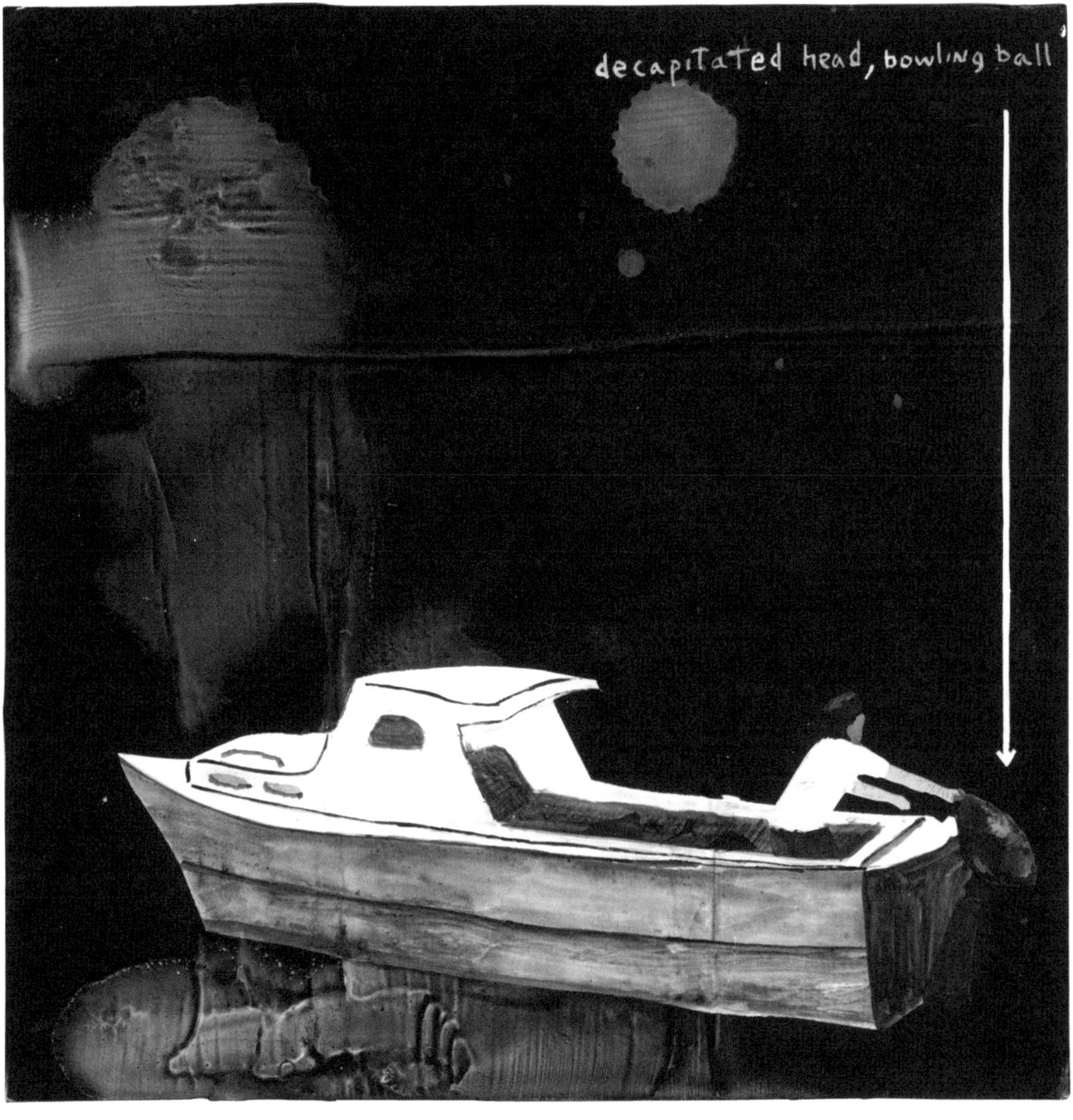
decapitated head, bowling ball

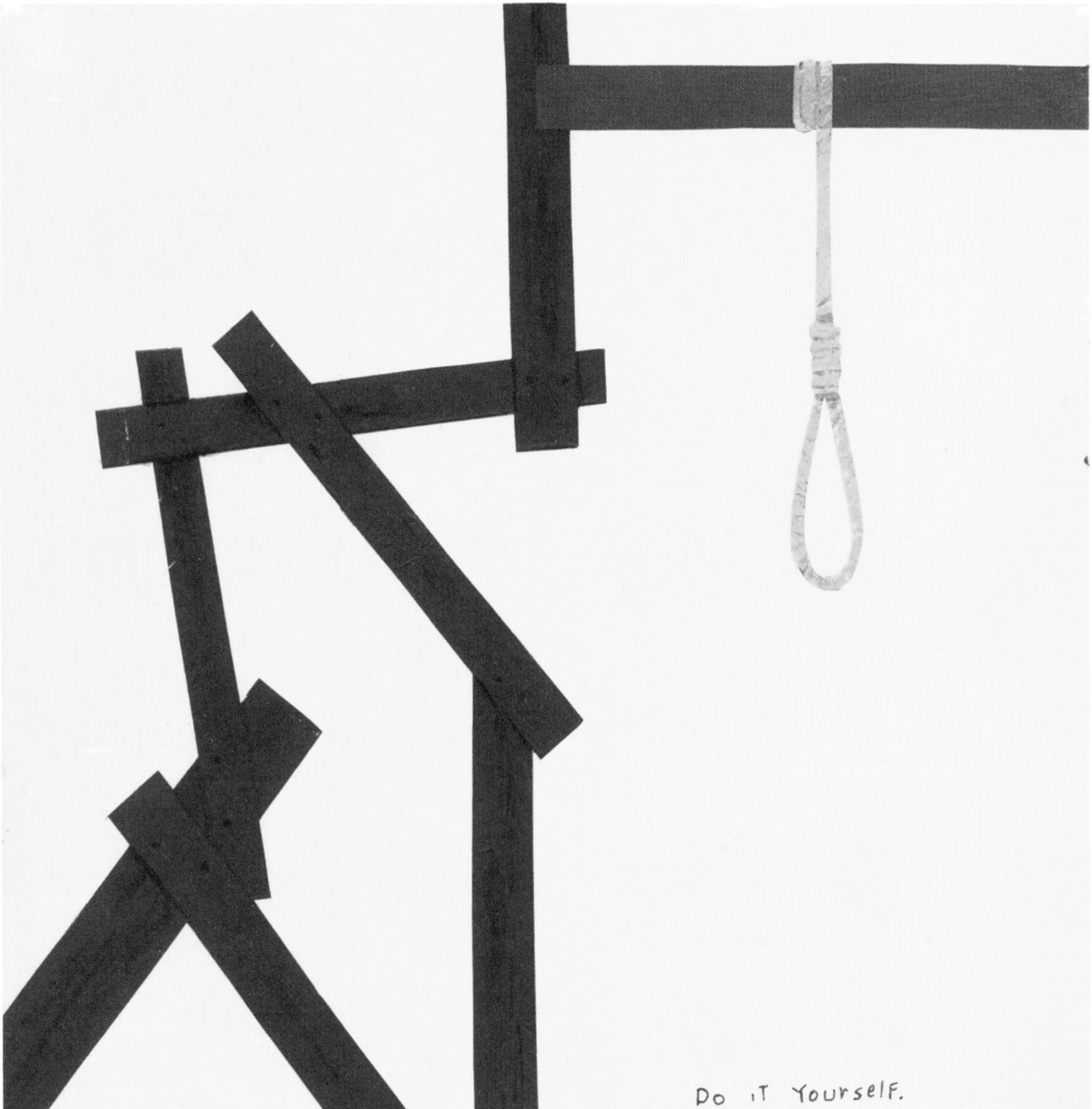
Do iT Yourself.

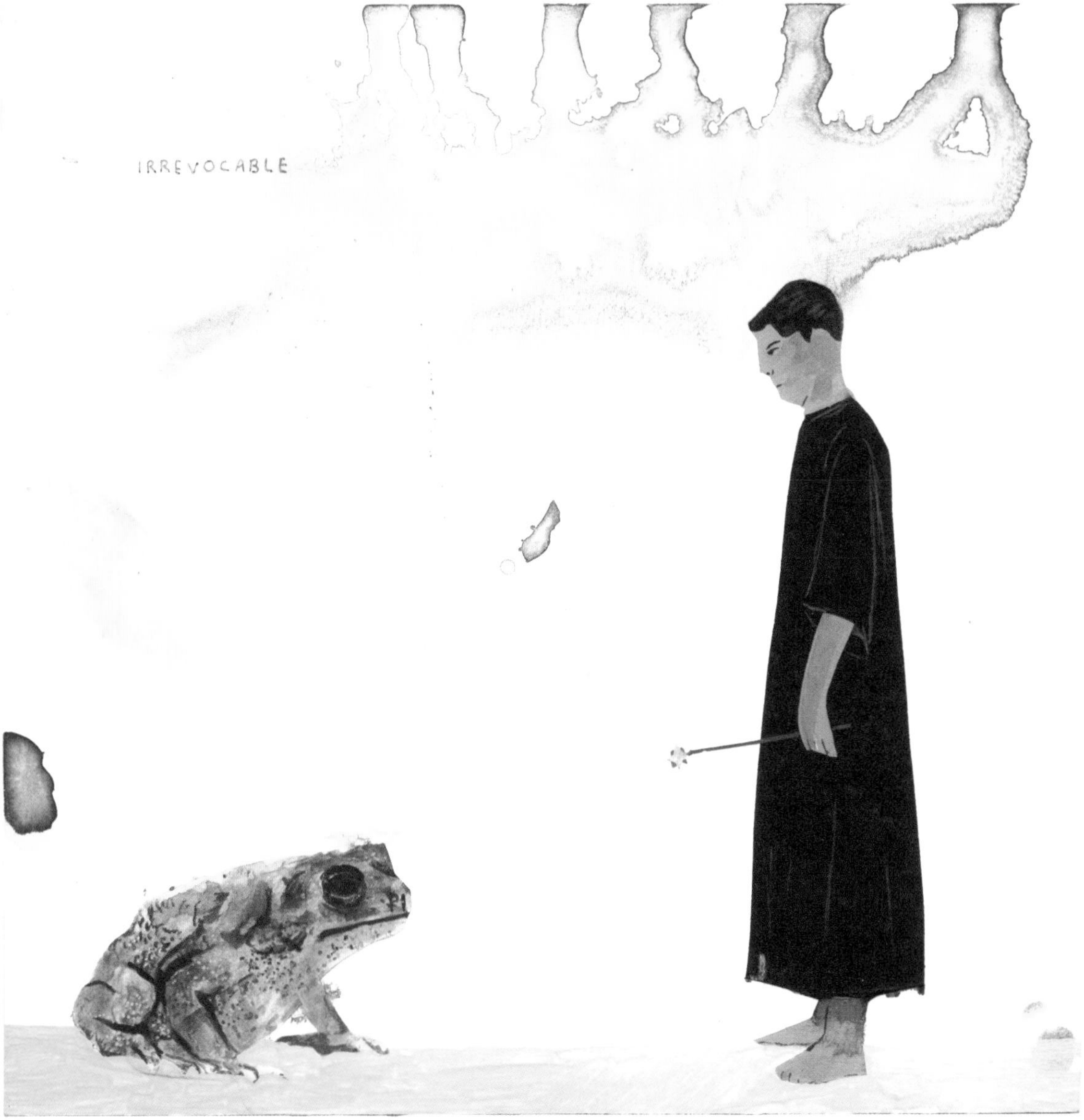
IRREVOCABLE

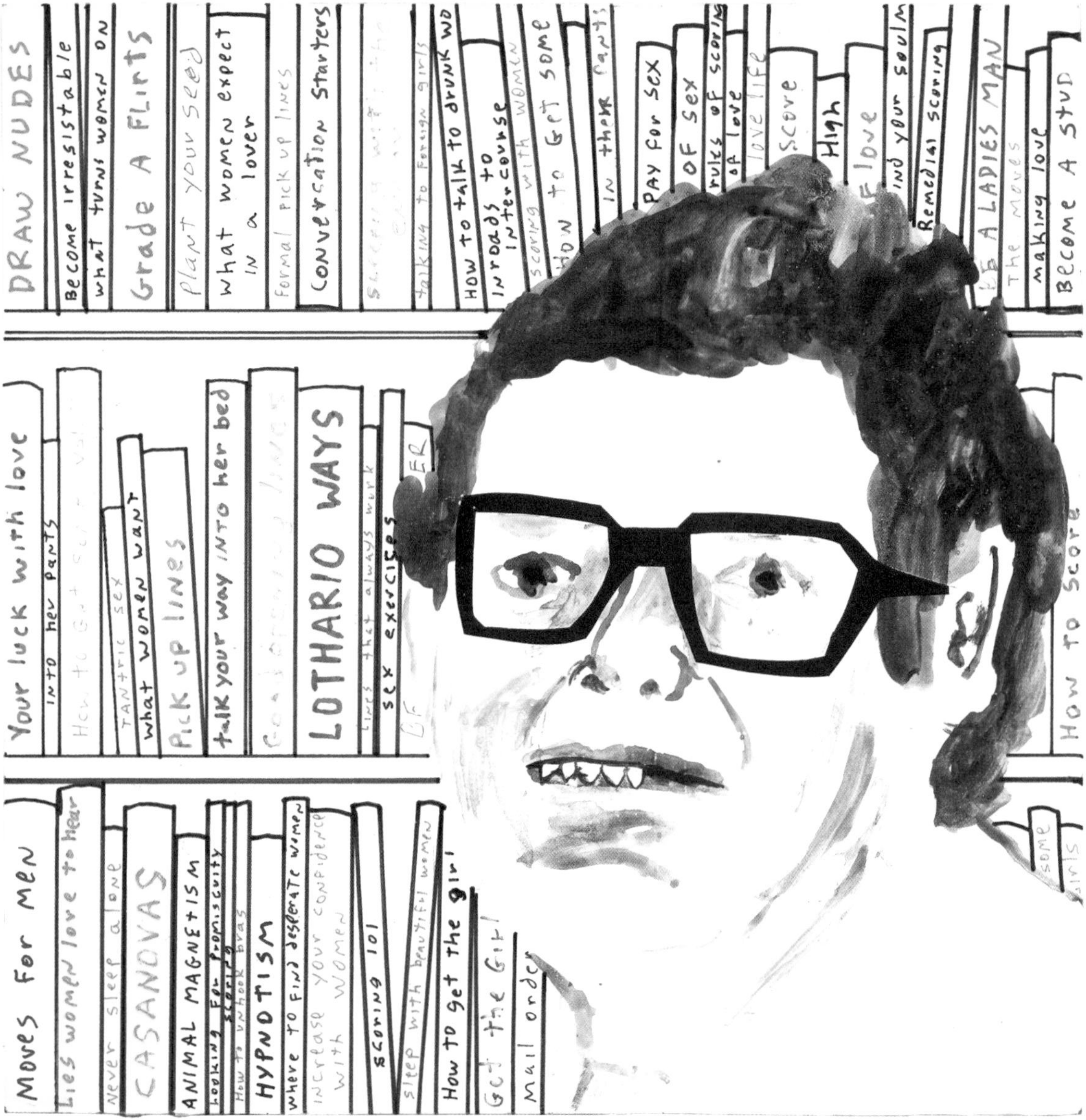
DRAW NUDES
Become irresistable
what turns women on
Grade A Flirts
plant your seed
what women expect in a lover
Formal pick up lines
Conversation Starters
talking to foreign girls
How to talk to drunk wo
Inroads to intercourse
scoring with women
How to Get some
In their pants
Pay for sex
of sex
rules of scoring
of love
love life
Score
High
love
ind your soulm
Remedial scoring
A LADIES MAN
The moves
making love
Become a stud
Your luck with love
into her pants
Tantric sex
what women want
Pick up lines
talk your way into her bed
LOTHARIO WAYS
Lines that always work
sex exercises
How to score
Moves for men
Lies women love to hear
never sleep alone
CASANOVAS
ANIMAL MAGNETISM
looking for promiscuity
scoring
How to unhook bras
HYPNOTISM
where to find desperate women
increase your confidence with women
scoring 101
sleep with beautiful women
How to get the girl
Get the Girl
Mail order
some

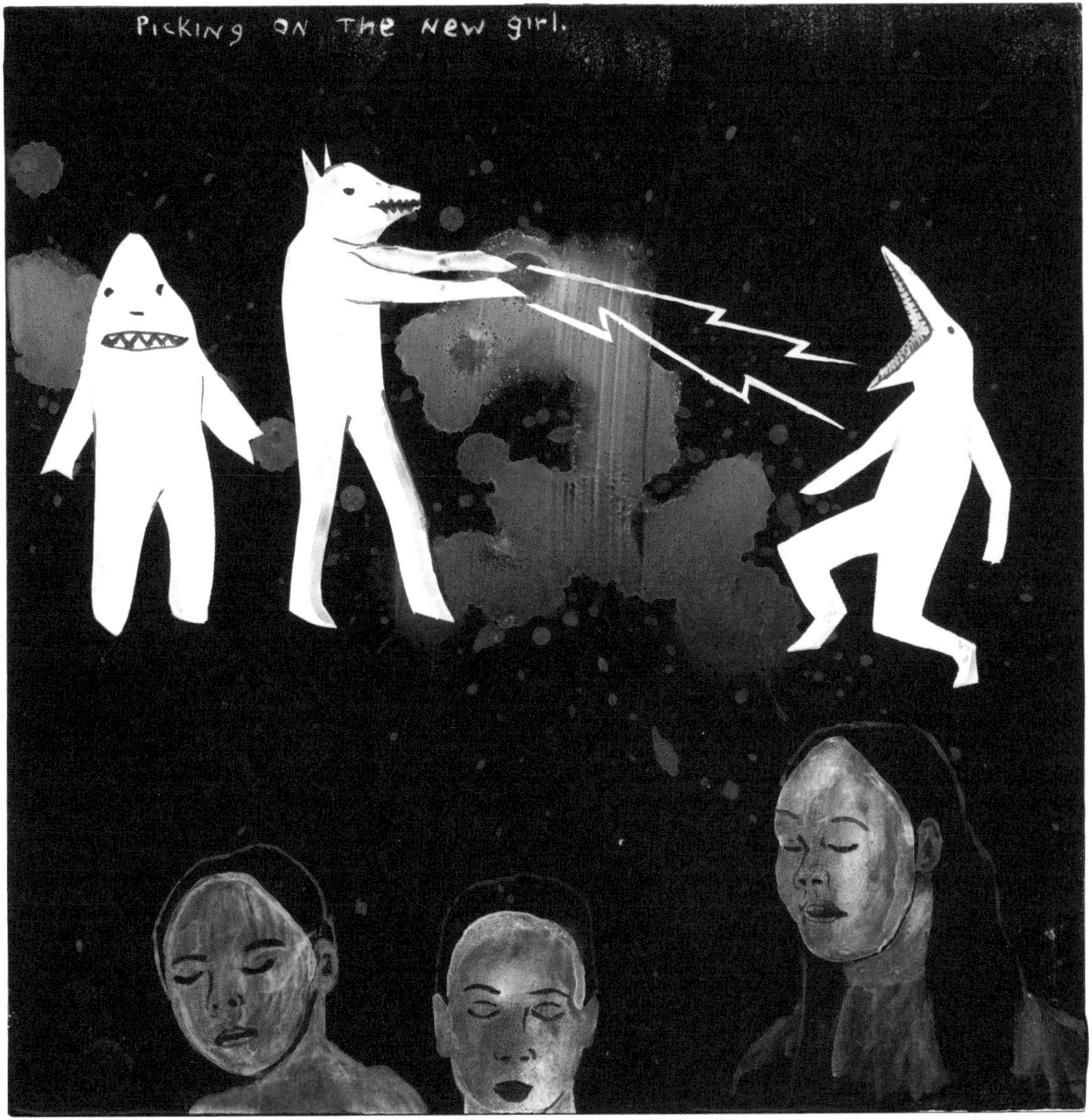
Picking on the new girl.

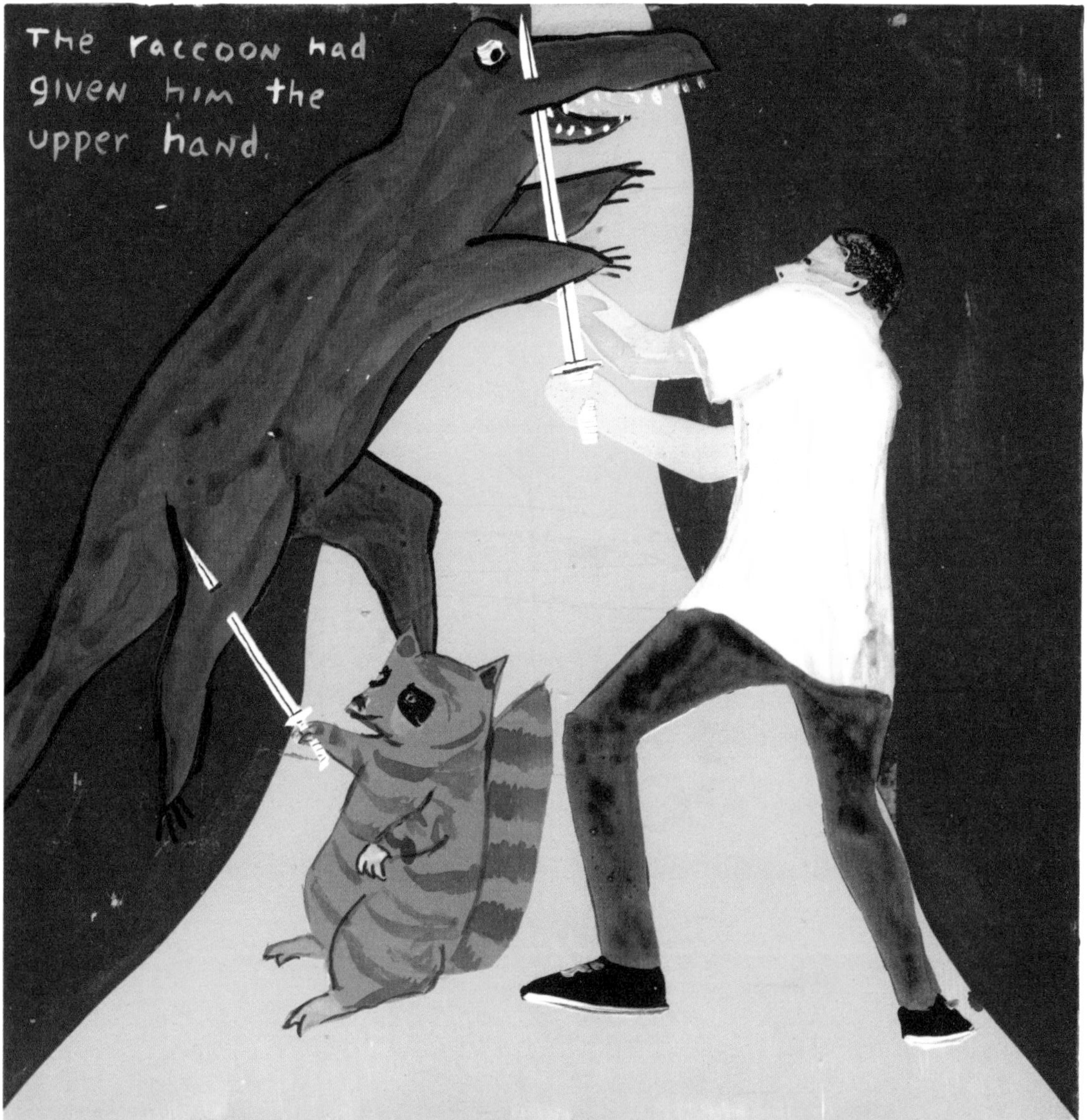
The raccoon had
given him the
upper hand.

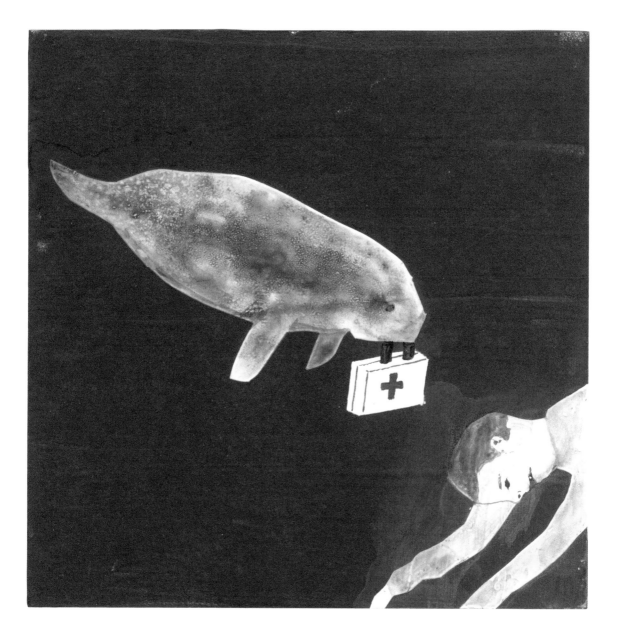

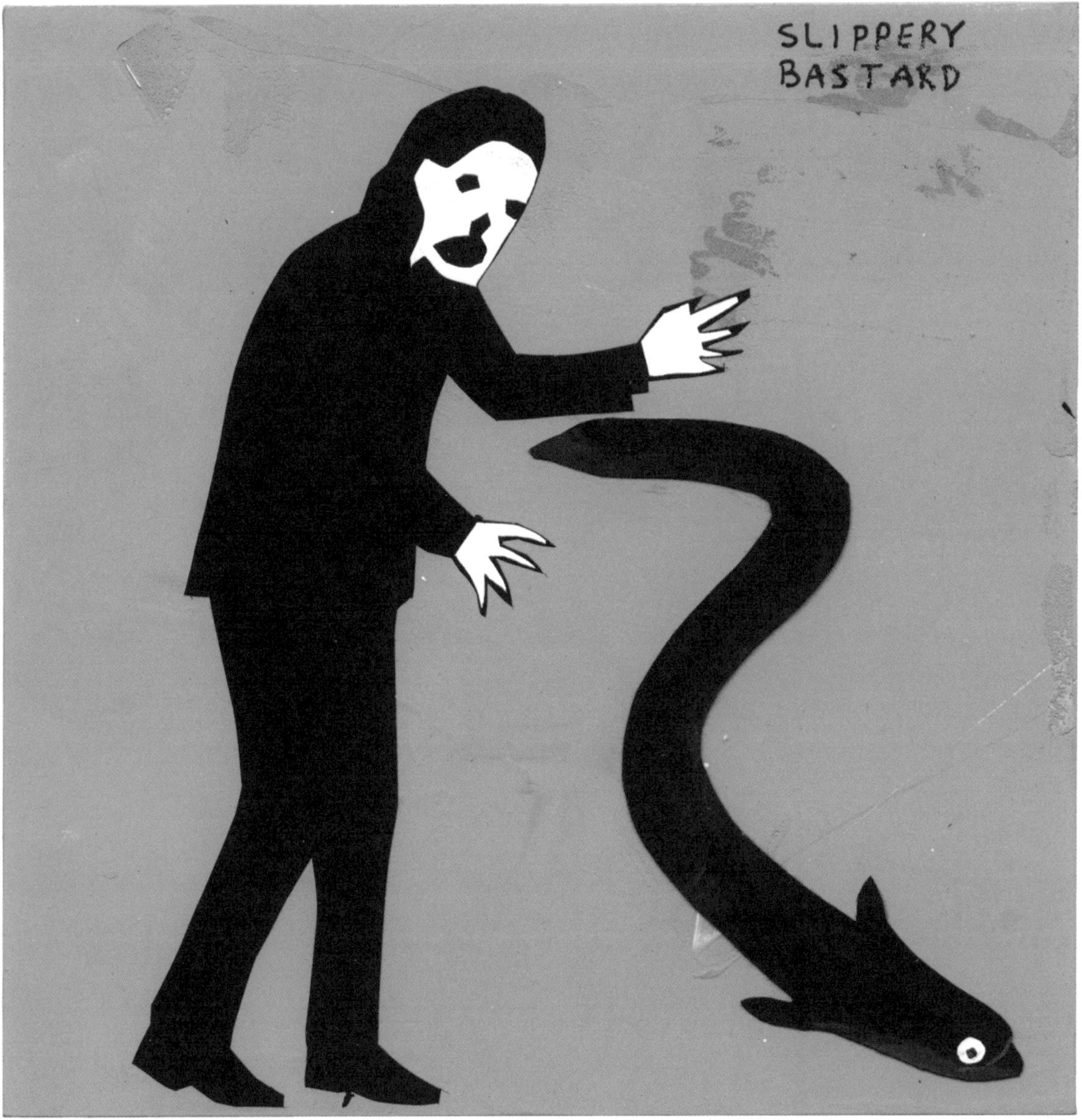
SLIPPERY
BASTARD

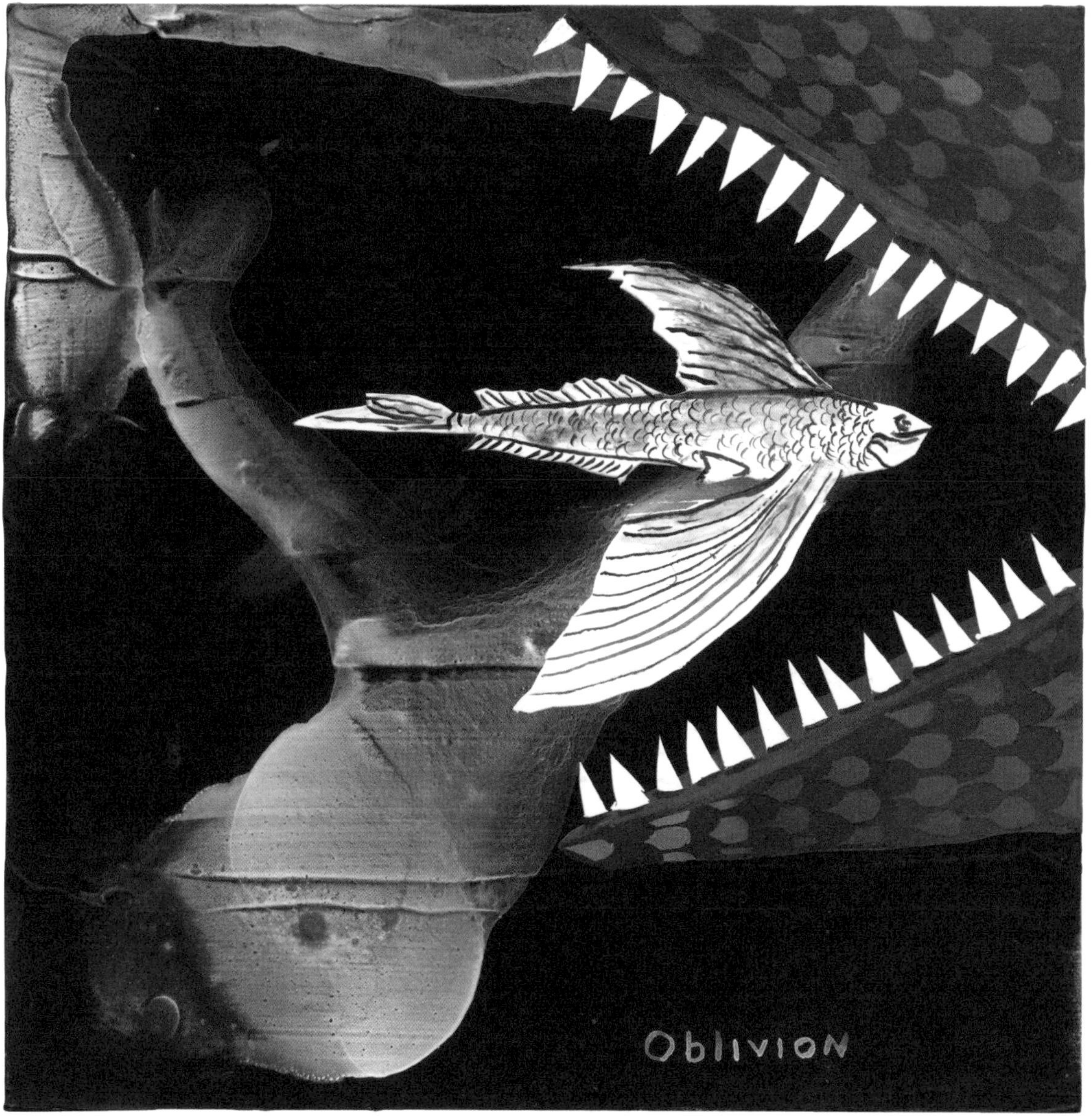
Oblivion

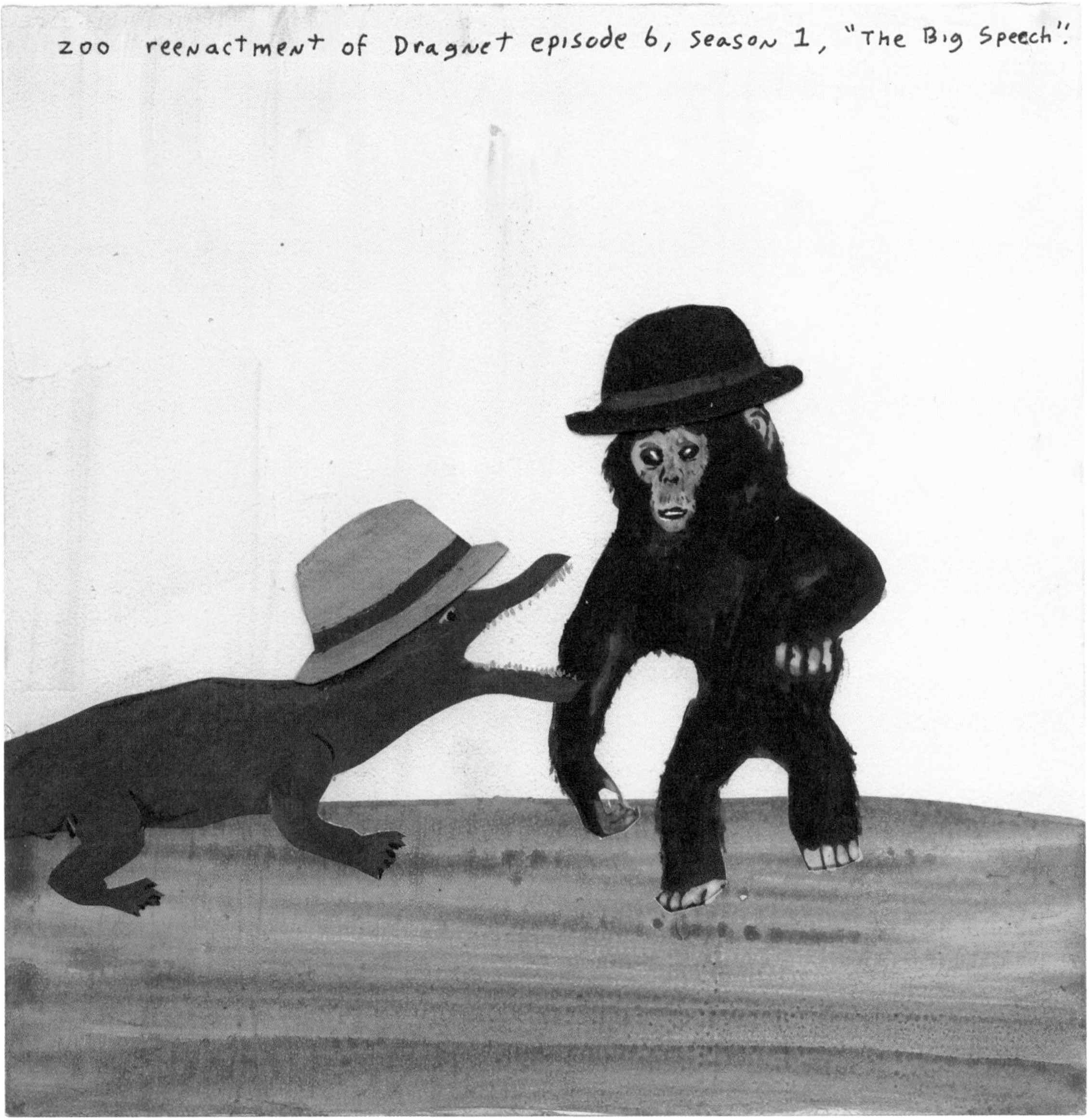
zoo reenactment of Dragnet episode 6, season 1, "The Big Speech".

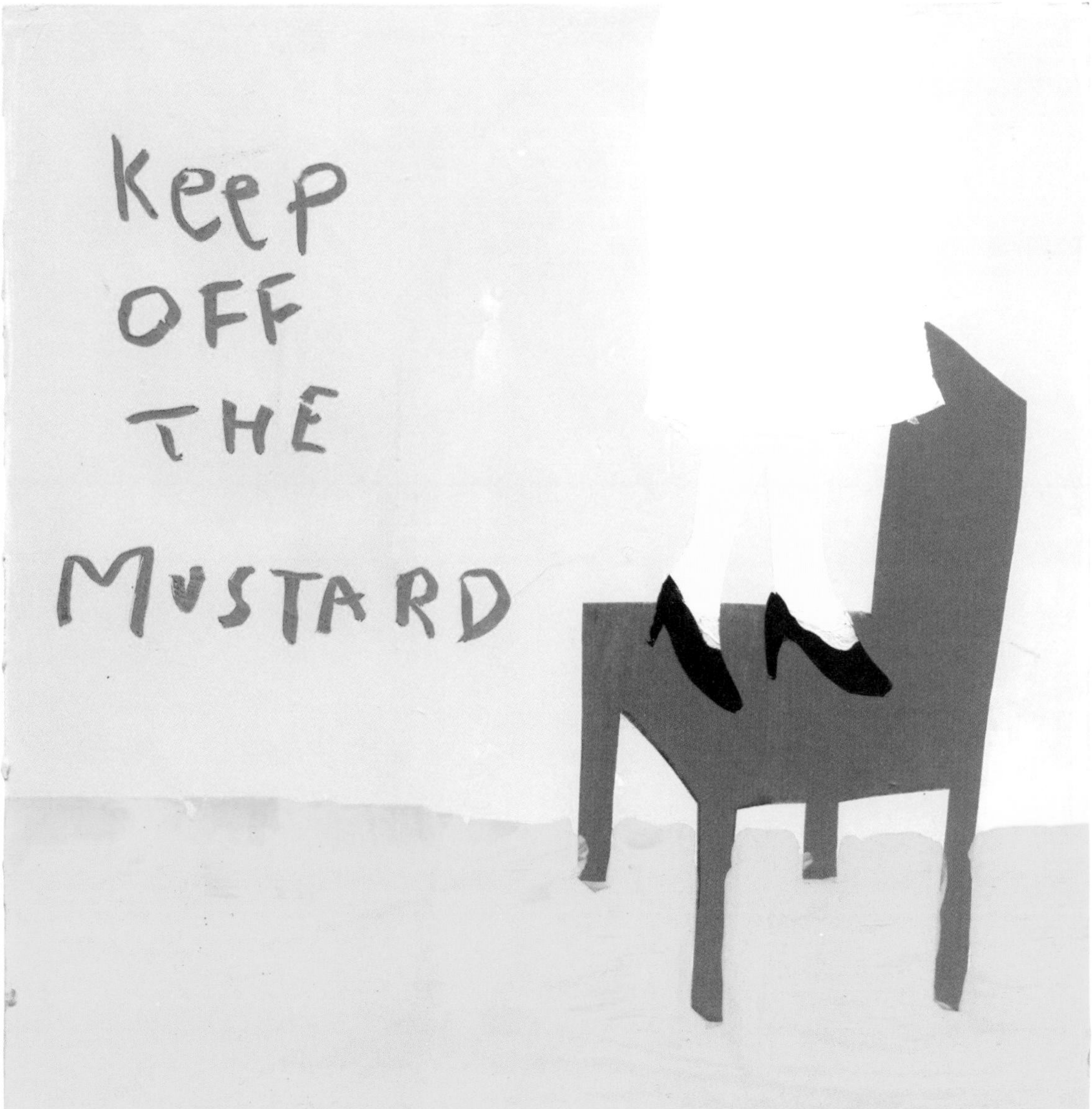
KEEP
OFF
THE
MUSTARD

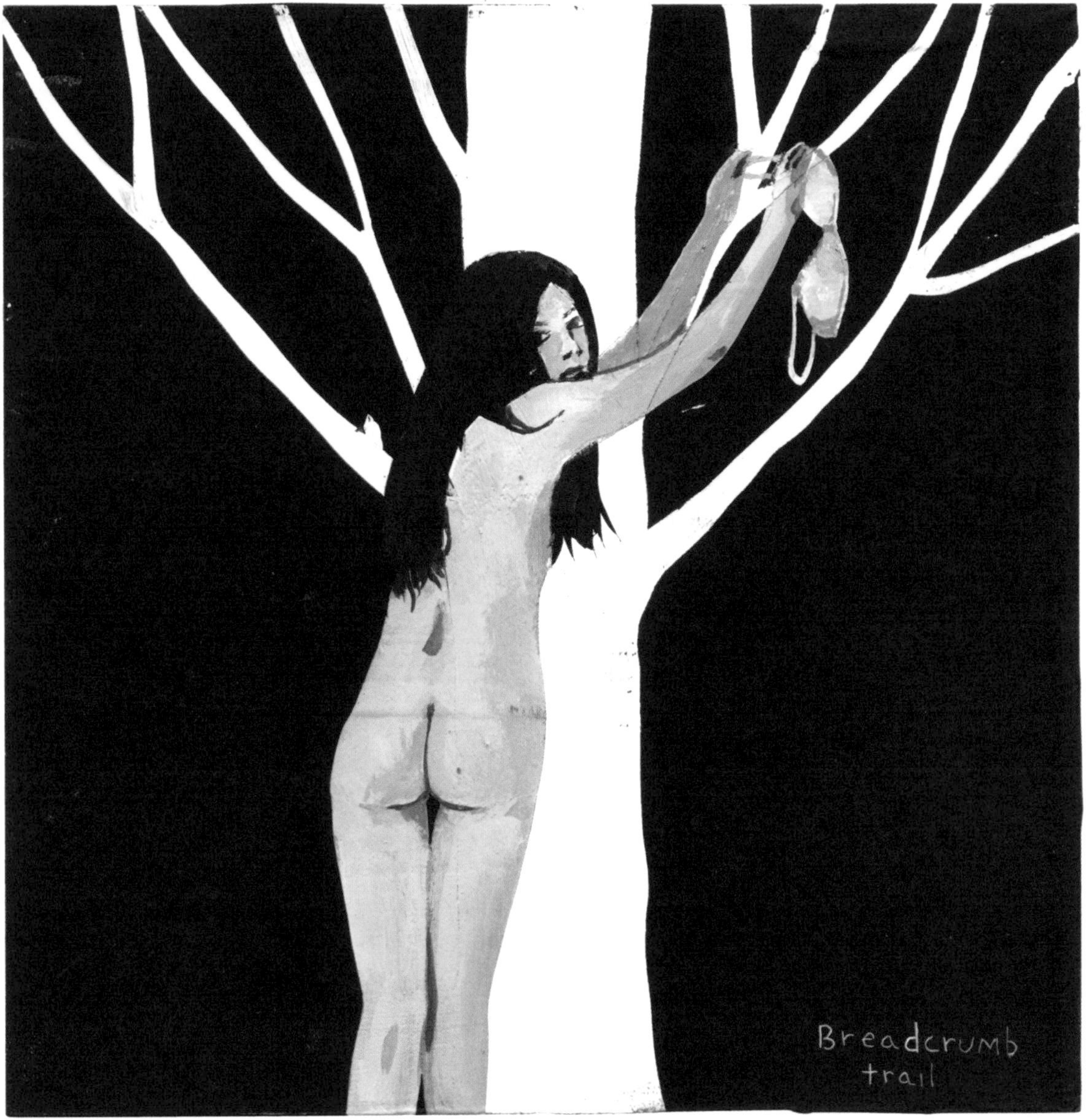
Breadcrumb
trail

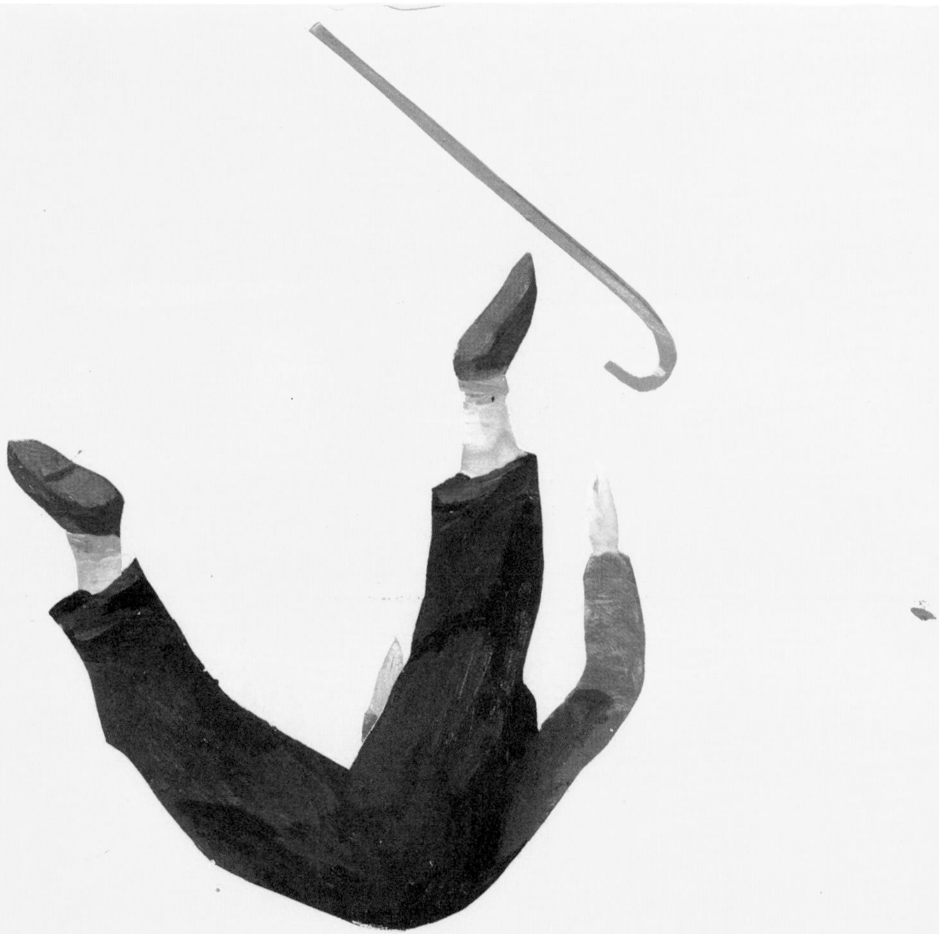

GRAMPOLINE

Soup of the day
Cabbage roll soup
Salad of the day
Cabbage rolls

Making memories that last a lifetime.

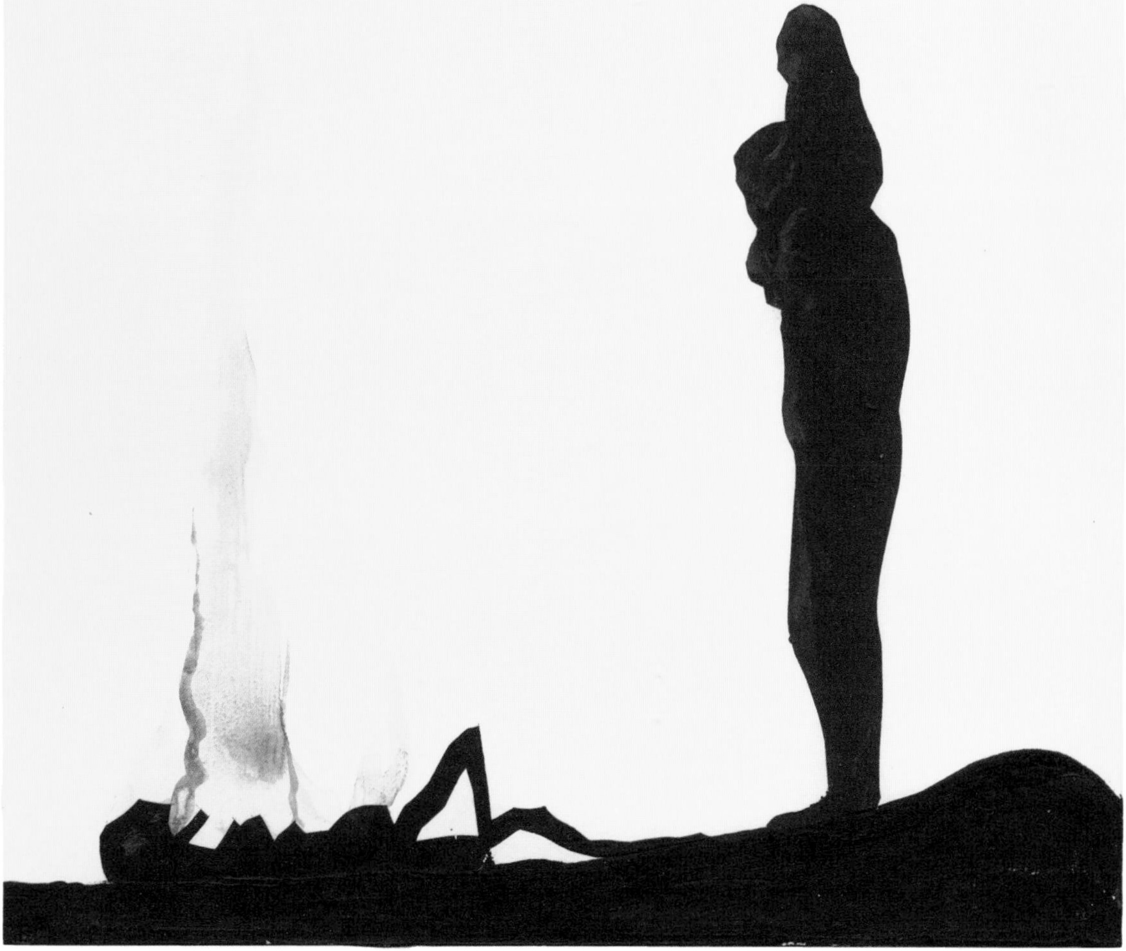

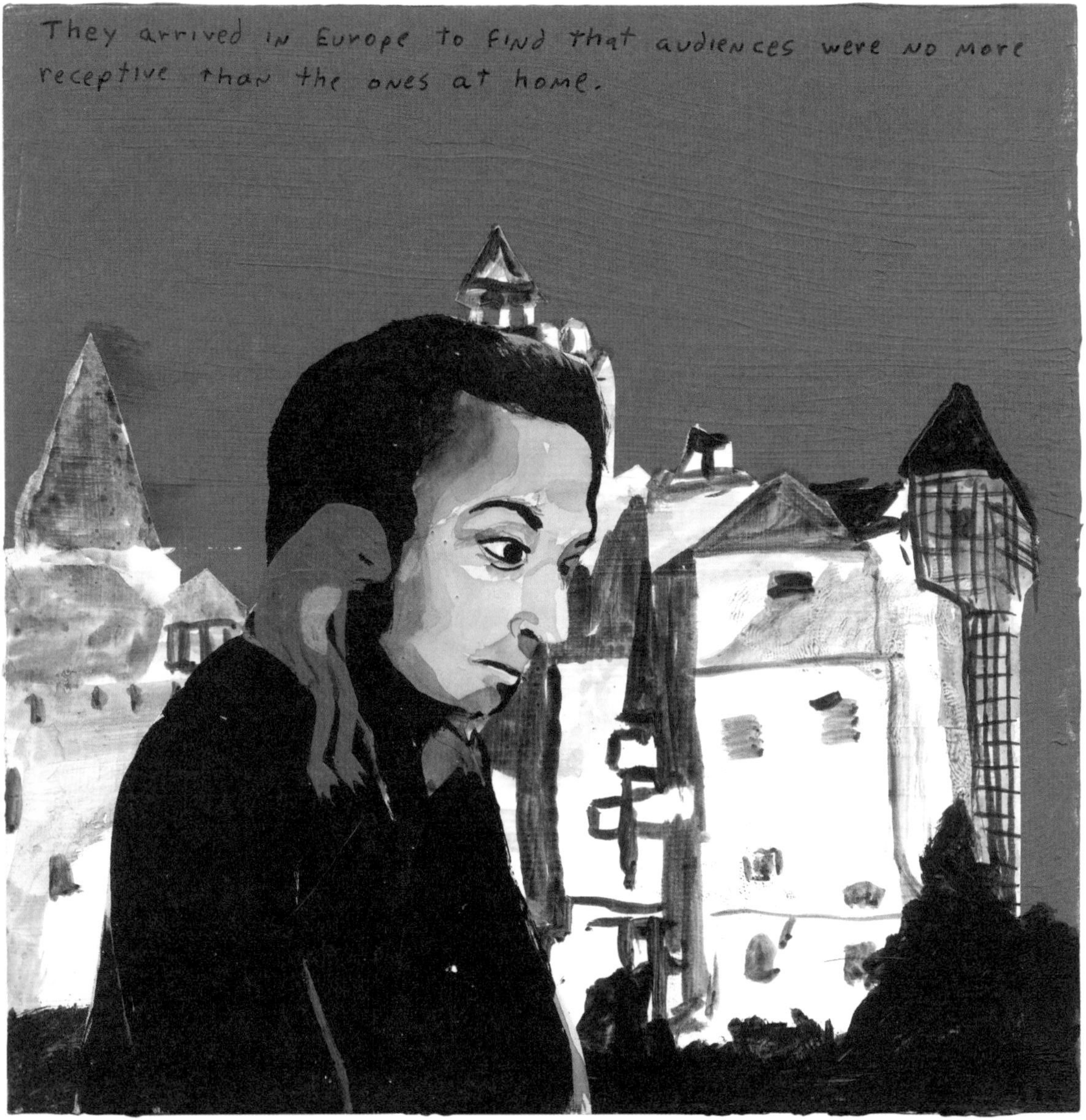
They arrived in Europe to find that audiences were no more receptive than the ones at home.

FLOODED AND BLINDED

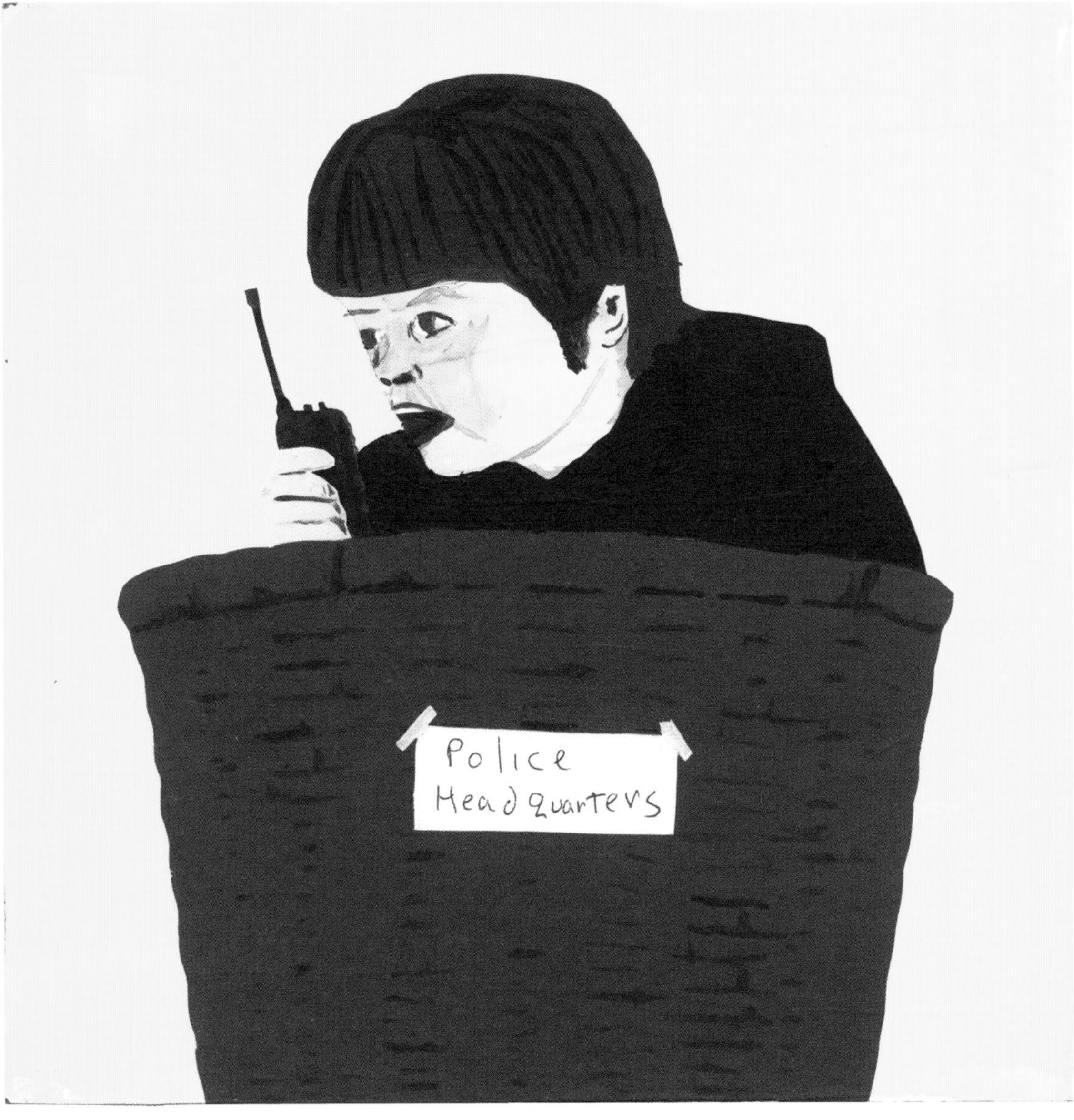
Police
Headquarters

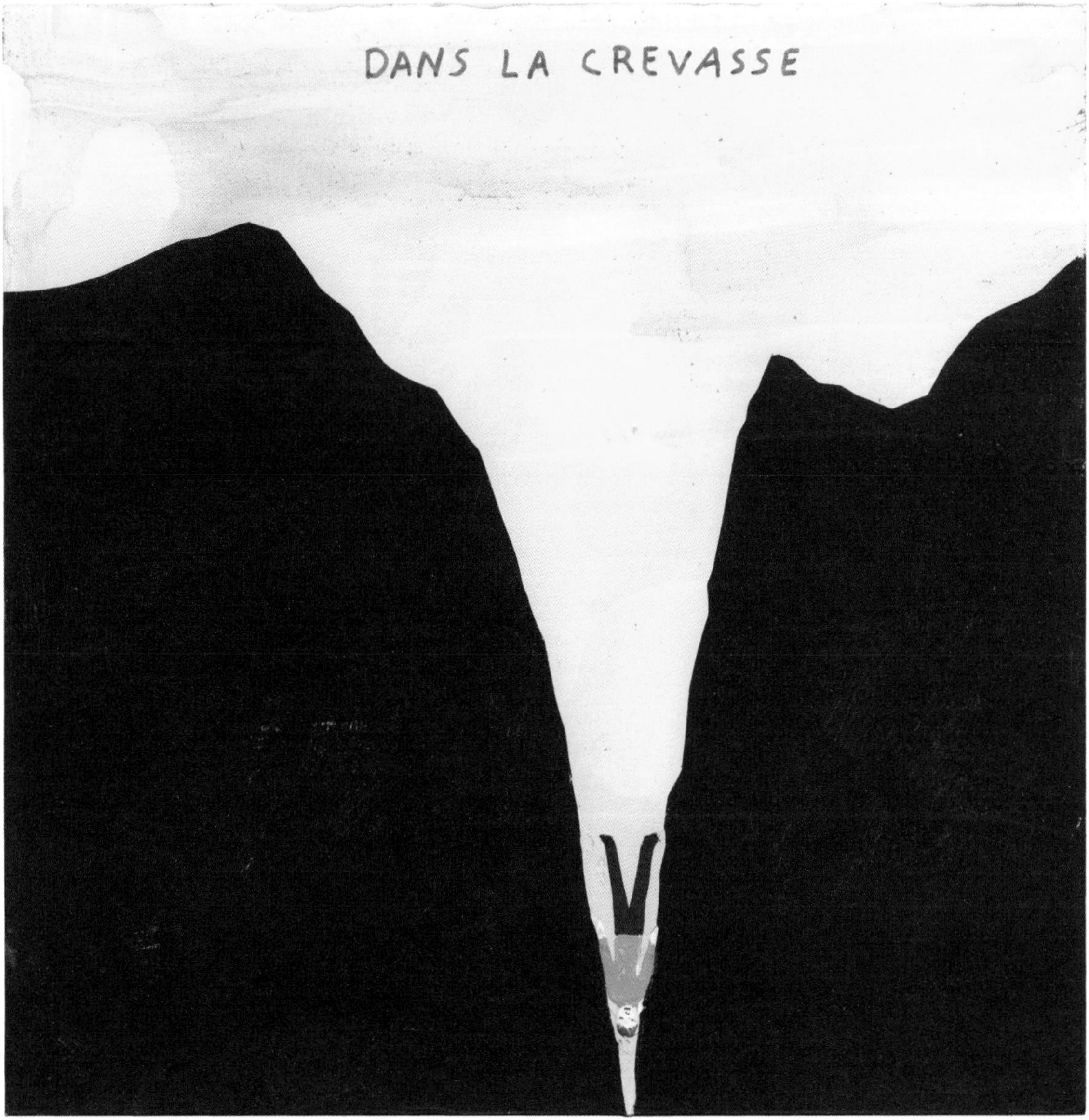
DANS LA CREVASSE

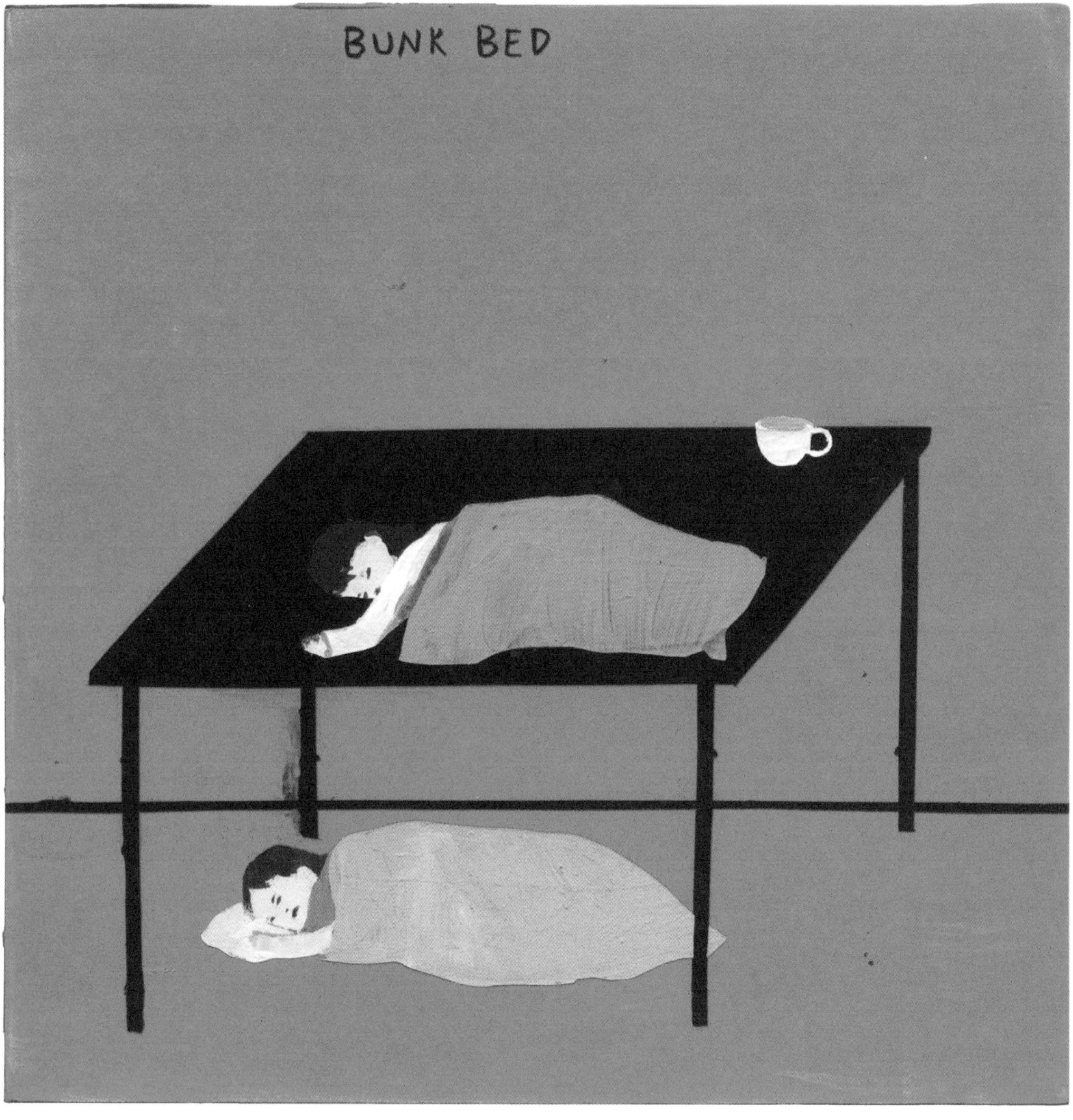
BUNK BED

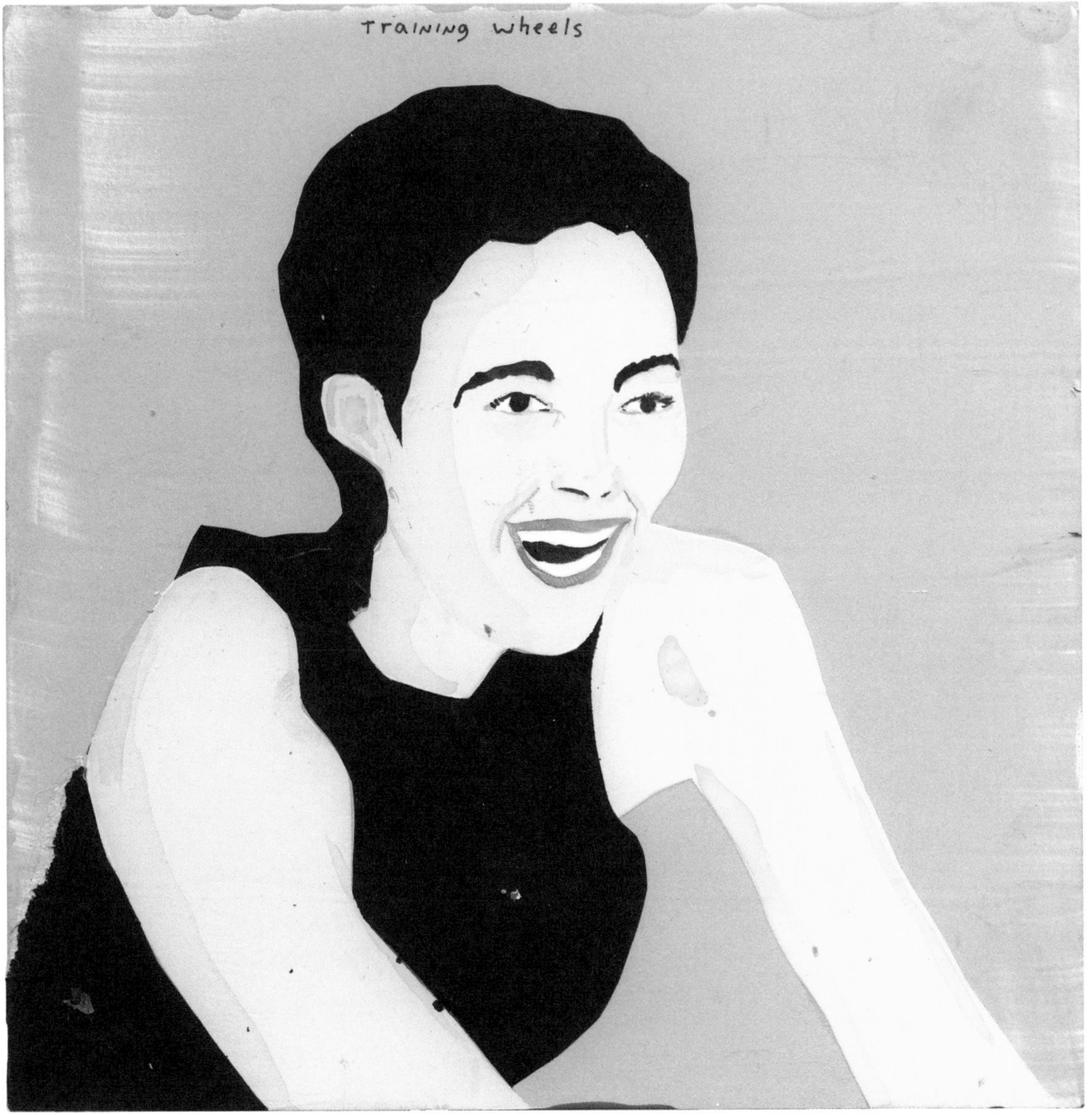
training wheels

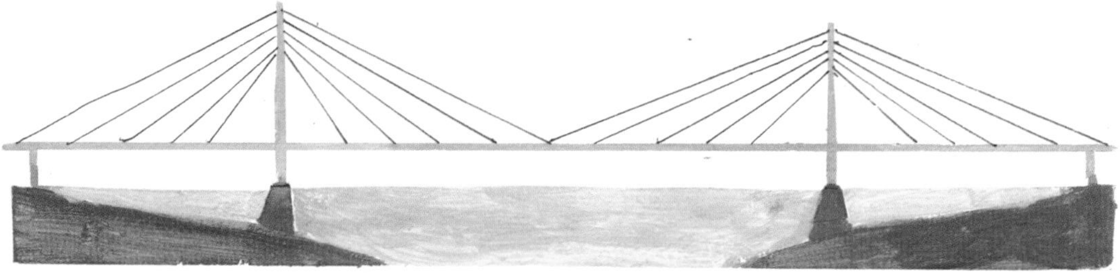

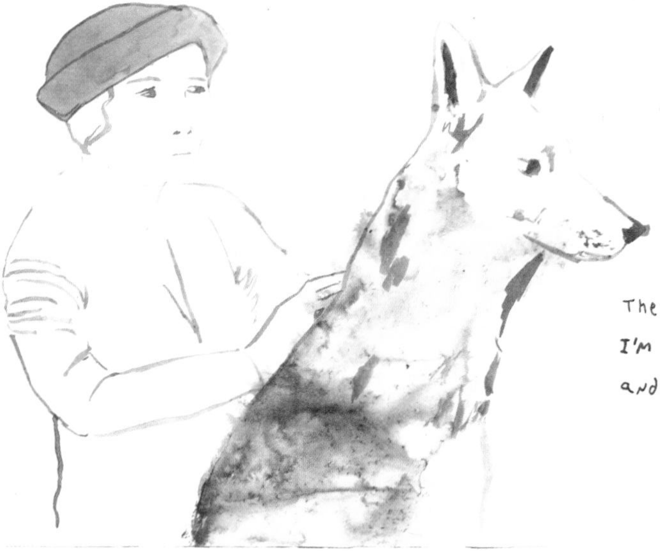

The second she lets go,
I'm over that bridge
and gone.

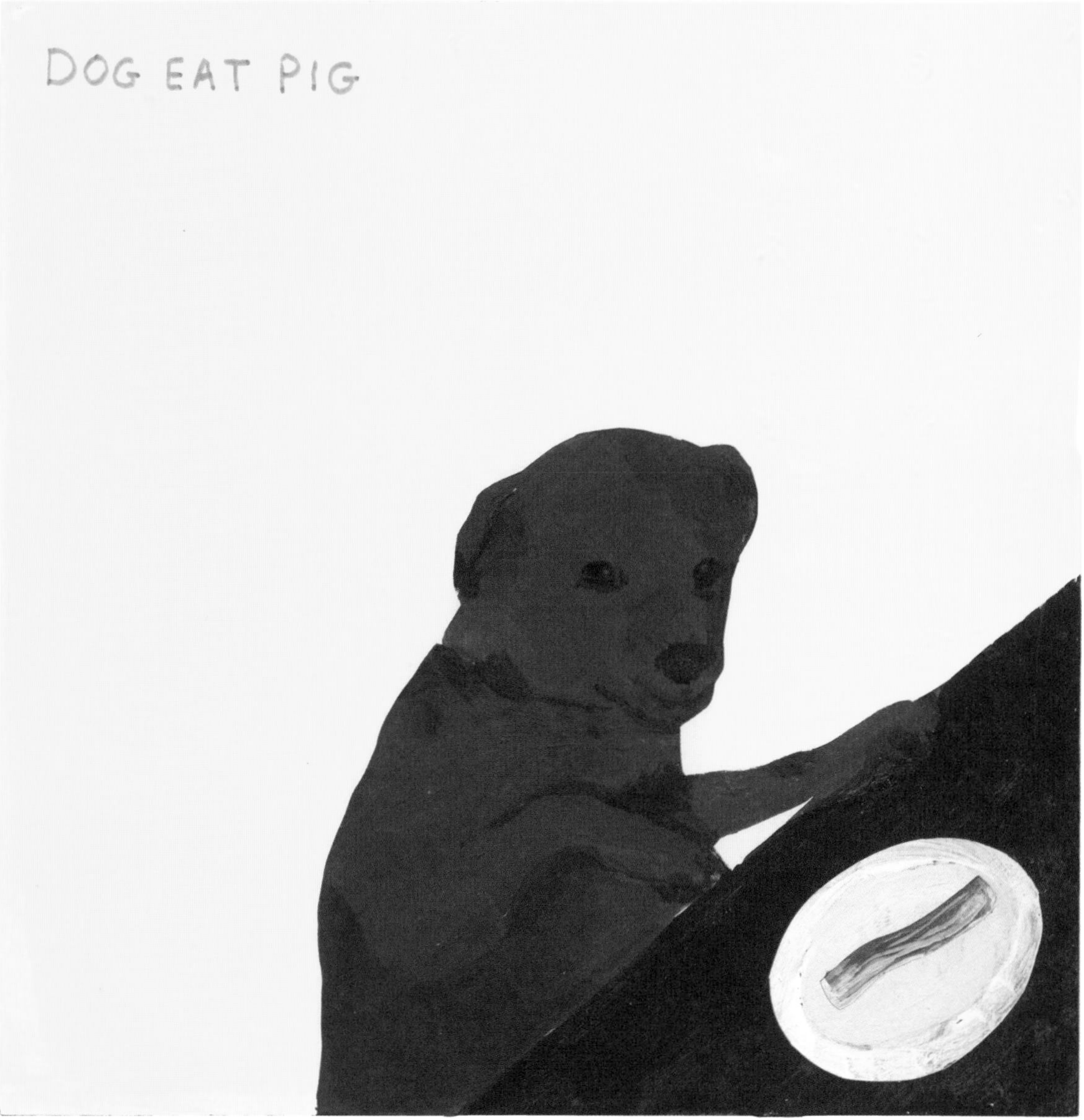
DOG EAT PIG

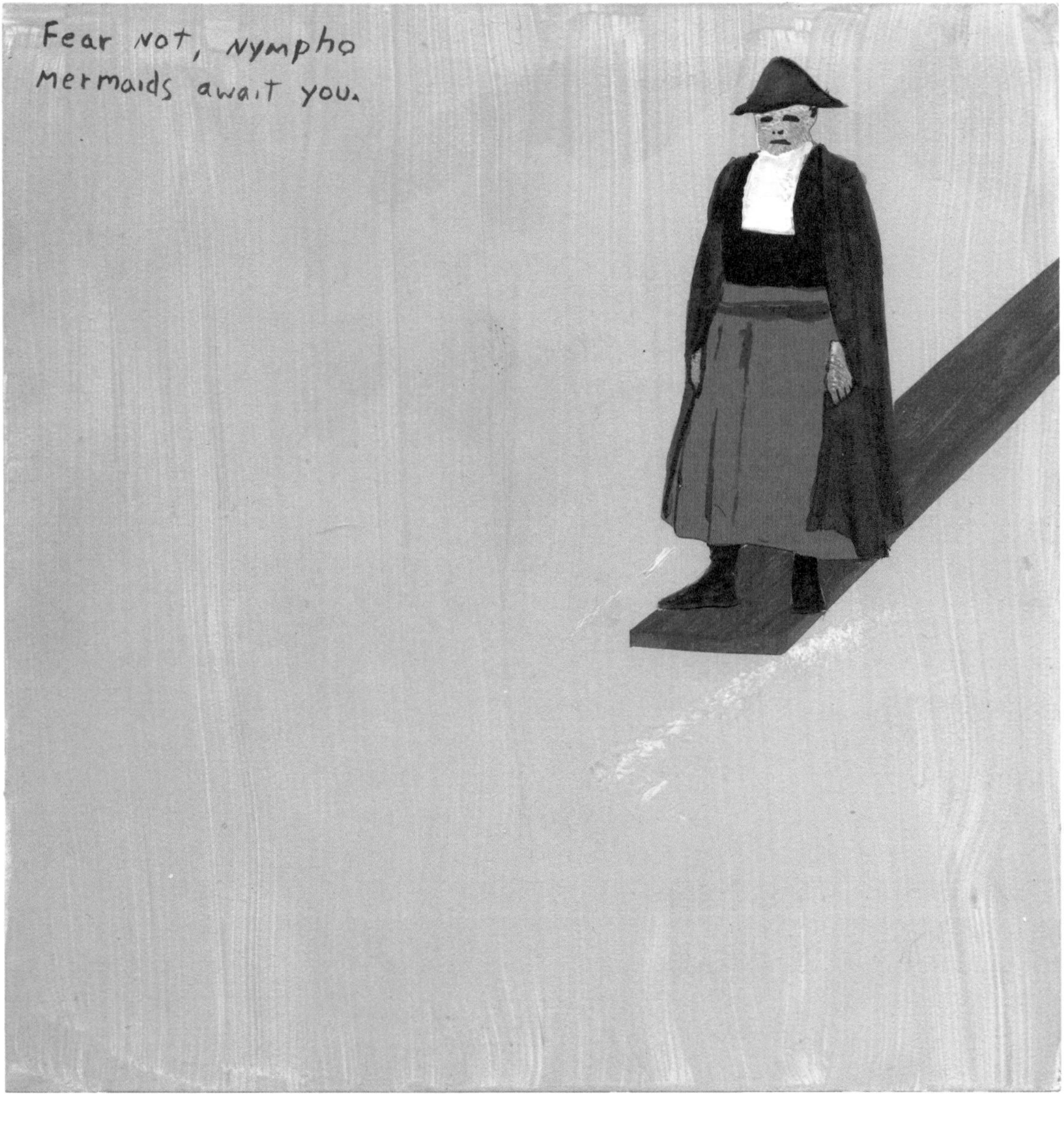
Fear not, nympho
mermaids await you.

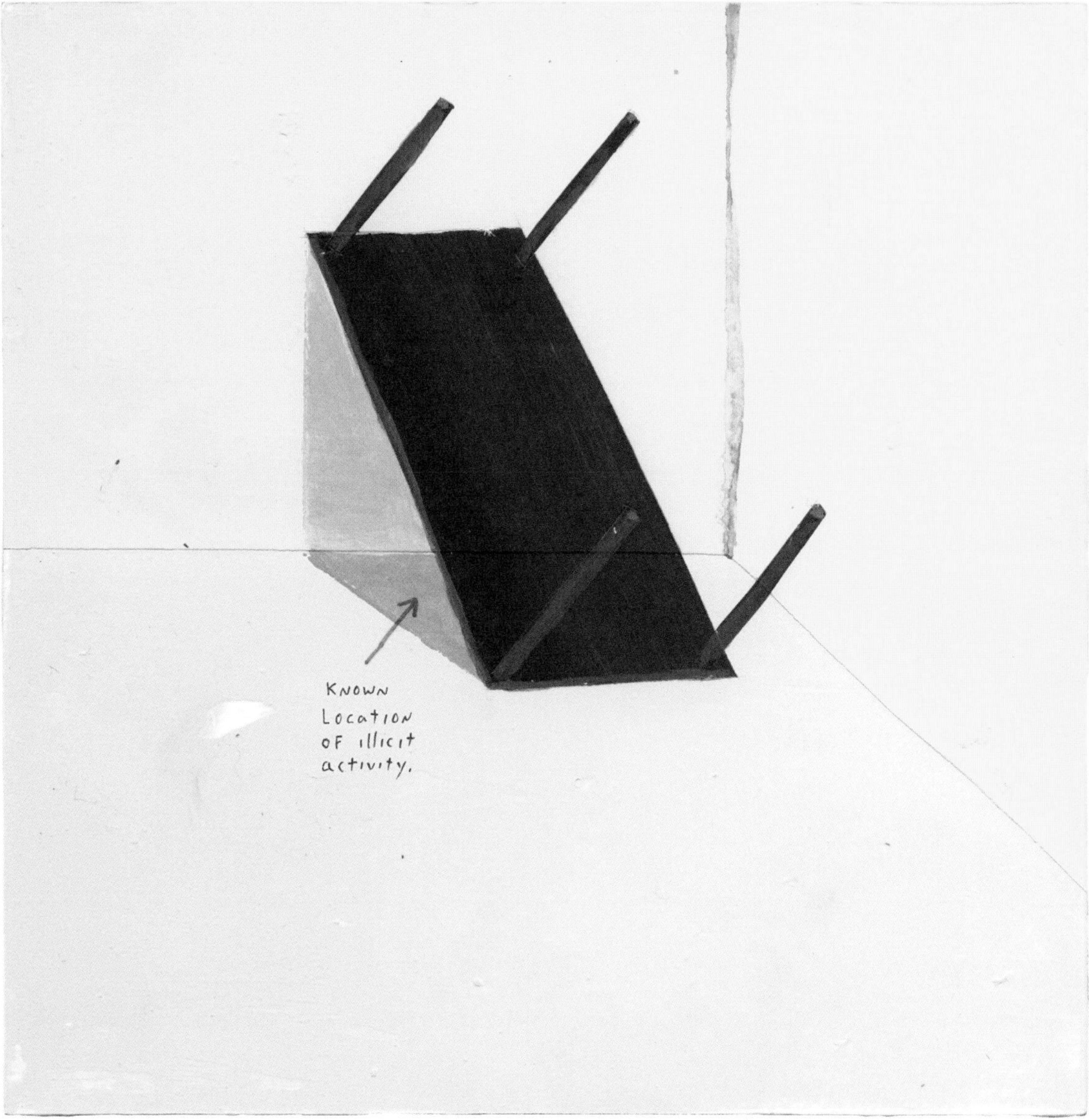
KNOWN
Location
OF illicit
activity.

(S)love(n)ly Art

Before the platonic Big Bang, men and women were undivided solid spheres. After the fall, they endlessly searched for their missing part, aiming to reunite without hope.

Similarly, there was a time and place when Words and Things were One. Chased out of Eden by a flaming Swiss Army knife, they now live a lusty, miserable existence: locking themselves in barbed-wired enclaves, fighting wars, making love in straight or perverted ways.

Michael Dumontier and Neil Farber run a *Motel next to the Swamp*: in its rooms strange couples meet. Icons and Texts interact in different forms, carefully planned in weeks or rapidly consumed in a blind date fashion. Their mode of intercourse includes solitude, shy eye-gazes, arm-on-shoulder approaches, bedside dramas, voyeurism, beastly behaviours, bondage.

Their attires are usually dowdy, their manners slovenly; they seek a temporary love, or the illusion of it.

Icons cannot speak, Texts cannot see. They just stay close, touch, feel. Sometimes they don't match, or don't even recognize each other; they know their relationship will have no future.

Yet, they adore to tease each other, to test the magnetic fields generated by particles flowing along intersecting orbits.

From time to time, Love arises for no reason or rhyme.

Their square room, its acrylic-painted masonite walls,

becomes Heaven.

–Cino Zucchi

Michael Dumontier and **Neil Farber** *met while students at the University of Manitoba. In March 1996, they helped found the Royal Art Lodge collective and remained active members until the group disbanded in 2008. Since that time, they have continued to work together, meeting once a week to make collaborative paintings. At the same time, Michael and Neil maintain their own independence. They live and work in Winnipeg, Manitoba.*

Cino Zucchi *is an architect and writer who lives and works in Milan, Italy.*